Michael Hviid Jacobsen

(editor)

PUBLIC SOCIOLOGY

– Proceedings of the Anniversary Conference
Celebrating Ten Years of Sociology in Aalborg

AALBORG UNIVERSITY PRESS

2008

Public Sociology
– Proceedings of the Anniversary Conference
Celebrating Ten Years of Sociology in Aalborg
Michael Hviid Jacobsen (editor)

© The Authors and Aalborg University Press, 2008

Cover: Særpræg Aps
Layout: Lars Pedersen / Anblik Grafisk

Printed by Narayana Press
ISBN-13: 978-87-7307-933-1

Distribution:
Aalborg University Press
Niels Jernes Vej 6B
9220 Aalborg
Denmark
Phone: (+45) 99 40 71 40, Fax: (+45) 96 35 00 76
E-mail: aauf@forlag.aau.dk

www.forlag.aau.dk

All rights reserved. No part of this book may be reprinted or reproduced or utilized in any form or by any electronic, mechanical, or other means, now known or hereafter invented, including photocopying and recording, or in any information storage or retrieval system, without permission in writing from the publishers, except for reviews and short excerpts in scholarly publications.

List of Content

PREFACE		5
INTRODUCTION	Public Sociology – Towards a Triple Hermeneutic *Michael Hviid Jacobsen*	7
CHAPTER 1	The Fall of Public Sociology *Ottar Brox*	57
CHAPTER 2	Making Sociology Matter – Phronetic Sociology as Public Sociology *Bent Flyvbjerg*	77
CHAPTER 3	Public Sociology – Models of Relevance for the 21st Century *James B. Rule*	119
CHAPTER 4	Pluralism and Critique – Public Sociology versus Academic Sociology *Henrik Dahl*	141
CHAPTER 5	The Media as Public – The Appearance of Sociology in the Media Environment *Keith Tester*	155
RECOMMENDED READING	Public Sociology as Subject Matter of Sociology *Michael Hviid Jacobsen*	179
LIST OF CONTRIBUTORS		185

PREFACE

In recent years, sociology has – by numerous stakeholders in society – increasingly been requested or expected to be public or to prove its public worth and relevancy – its relevance and contribution to the outside world, to various groups within society, to science, to our general stock of knowledge or to governmental agencies funding sociological educational programs and research projects. Within the discipline itself, we have also witnessed the rise of a continuous debate dealing with the public nature – or public possibilities, responsibilities, priorities, commitments and obligations – of sociology which has now been waging and raging for some years. This debate – coupled with the specific mentality of the Sociology Program at Aalborg University with its problem-based learning, its group work model, its project pedagogy and its publicly oriented research profile – inspired us to dedicate our tenth year anniversary conference to the topic of public sociology.

This book consists of a collection of originally orally delivered presentations from a host of nationally and internationally acclaimed sociologists. I am thankful to these people, whom we can now also call friends, who took their time and energy to come to Aalborg and share their ideas and visions with us and subsequently to compose the inspirational chapters included in this volume. Also thanks to all the many participants making our anniversary conference memorably days. But I wish especially to extend my gratitude to those involved in planning and directing the conference – Maria Libak Pedersen, Julie Nygaard Pedersen, Janne Sverd, Mette Rytter Christensen, Rasmus Antoft, Gunnar Scott Reinbacher, Jens Tonboe, Anja Jørgensen, Sune Qvotrup Jensen and Antje Gimmler whose energetic efforts made it all possible. Finally, I also wish to extend my gratitude to those invited guests giving stimulating and thought-provoking presentations in the many different workshops.

The conference and the subsequent publication of this volume have received financial support from several beneficiaries. I am very grateful for the support received from The Department of Sociology, Social Work & Organisation, The Social Science Faculty at Aalborg University, CASTOR, The C. W. Obel Foundation, The Department of History, International and Social Studies and finally from The Sociology Program. Without their generous financial support, our conference would probably never have taken place and this book would never have appeared – that is, it would have remained utterly unpublic. However, due to the kind support of our beneficiaries, the ideas presented at the conference became public. I also wish to thank Aalborg University Press for publishing the volume. It is my hope – and contention – that the chapters in the book may inspire the debate on and practice of public sociology for many years to come.

Michael Hviid Jacobsen
Director of Studies/Associate Professor
Aalborg University
Winter 2007/2008

PUBLIC SOCIOLOGY
- Towards a Triple Hermeneutic

~

Michael Hviid Jacobsen

> "Anyone who cannot be replaced by another – for the reason that he is unlike any other – is one who fulfils no undeniable need. So we find in the intellectual population these two remarkable categories: *intellectuals who serve some purpose* and *intellectuals who serve none*"
>
> – Paul Valéry, *History and Politics*

A SOCIOLOGY OF SOCIOLOGY

For decades it has been fashionable – especially among sociologists – to diagnose either the current or endemic crisis of sociology or to predict the imminent and irreversible downfall and dissolution of the discipline (see e.g. Bottomore 1975; Boudon 1980; Horowitz 1994; MacRae 1964; Stinchcombe 1994; Wolfe 1992). The reasons for this supposed downfall and the upsurge in recent gloomy diagnoses of the future of the discipline have been many and diversified and yet sociology – at least so far – has remained alive and kicking. It will be my claim in this introductory chapter on public sociology that the reason for sociology's continued survival, despite many premature symbolic burials, should be sought and found in sociology's continued relevance for and service to the public.

In his wonderful, yet in recent years increasingly overlooked book *The Social Role of the Man of Knowledge*, Florian Znaniecki posed the following relevant but also, as he admitted, rhetorical question:

> How can it be that scientists, men who indulge in cultivating knowledge instead of being effectively active like everybody else, are not only tolerated by men of action but granted a social status and regarded as performing a desirable social function by the communities in which they live? (Znaniecki 1940:23).

The answer to this tricky question should – I believe – be located in the fact that scientists, and in connection to the topic of this book especially sociologists, are regarded as serving a desirable social purpose that is recognized by the wider or general public or at least certain parts of it. Serving a purpose, a public purpose, is therefore not an inferior or derogatory raison d'être – it is, in fact, the lifeblood of sociology. Thus, it is only insofar that sociologists are capable of appealing to or assisting the general public or parts of it in relation to some problems, projects or grievances that they may, eventually, be tolerated and granted status, recognition and social function by the communities in which the live and work.

And true, there are to my knowledge hardly any living sociologist hoping that his or her work will have no affect whatsoever on social reality or will be of no relevance to other people. However, there are many different ways of believing and proving that one's sociological work is useful, relevant, desired, workable, demanded or indeed helpful. Therefore, the idea or notion of 'public sociology', in the singular, is greatly misleading whereas 'public sociologies', in the plural, point to the fact that there are many ways to practice public sociology. Also, the idea of 'public sociology' (in quotation marks) is itself – as I will show later – in danger of becoming yet another academic fad in sociology with no relevance to the public.

The debate on public sociology sweeping across the discipline with heretofore unseen ferocity in these years is, however, far from new. It is part and parcel of what has, from time to time, been described as 'sociology of sociology' (see e.g. Friedrichs 1970; Reynolds & Reynolds 1970). The sociology of sociology is aimed at dissecting the discipline of sociology from the perspective of sociology, it is about using sociology itself as a field of research, it is about turning the discipline's inquisitive mentalities and peeping eyes inwards. As such the constant self-reflection, self-criticism and self-flagellation is, I believe, an integral part of the whole project of sociology – because sociology is concerned with the *social as its subject matter*, the preoccupation with the *social relevance* of its endeavours that the discussion of public sociology has revived is and remains a constant presence among practicing sociologists. This is also one of the main reasons why sociology, by default or by design, finds itself in an exceptional situation within the world of the sciences – we have never heard of, and would probably find utterly absurd, any inventions such as 'the chemistry of chemistry', 'the physics of physics' or 'the astronomy of astronomy'. However, 'the sociology of sociology' seemingly makes perfect sense – and so, apparently, does also the notion of 'public sociology'. Very few would in fact demand or expect from physics, astronomy or mathematics that they should be 'public' (meaning publicly accessible, publicly accountable and publicly understandable) or that their frame of reference would be 'the general public'. Interestingly enough, this is being and has continuously been required by sociology – from the outside world as well as from within its own ranks. And perhaps this is – taking sociology's subject matter 'the social' into consideration – rather unsurprising. After all, sociology is, per definition, a dialogical discipline – we discuss and debate – almost endlessly – what we are doing, why, how, with whom, when and so on. We therefore have a constant dialogue going on with ourselves about our discipline but we also have an ongoing dialogue with the outside world.

So why is it that we discuss 'public sociology' at all if public sociology, when it comes down to it, is almost synonymous with sociology? Is it not just yet another example of the narcissistic navel-picking sociological obsession with its own academic status and identity? Or is it rather because sociology is so nauseatingly nervous and uncertain of its own scientific status, perhaps feels so unpleasantly inferior (see Machlup 1956), that it constantly needs reassurance from the public that the public needs it? Edmund Mokrzycki, for one, claimed that "sociology, together with related disciplines ... is in an exceptional position; it is a discipline in which the very status of being scientific is at stake" (Mokrzycki 1983:4). Perhaps there is some truth in this. Take, as another prominent example of this position, Thomas S. Kuhn who wondered at the nature and cause of so many sociological debates vis-à-vis the debates flourishing within their natural scientific counterparts when stating in *The Structure of Scientific Revolutions*:

> I was struck by the number and extent of the overt disagreement between social scientists over the nature of legitimate scientific problems and methods. Both history and acquaintance made me doubt that practitioners of the natural sciences possess firmer or more permanent answers to such questions than their colleagues in social science. Yet, somehow, the practice of astronomy, physics, chemistry or biology normally fails to evoke controversies over fundamentals that today often seem endemic among, say, psychologists or sociologists (Kuhn 1970:viii).

From within the ranks of the discipline of sociology itself, C. Wright Mills – always with a keen eye on the internal as well as external fault lines – observed a similar tendency for sociological confusion and controversy when stating:

> The study of man contains a greater variety of intellectual styles than any other area of cultural endeavour. How different social scientists go about their work, and what they aim to accomplish by it, often do not seem to

> have a common denominator ... Let us admit the case of our critics from the humanities and from the experimental sciences: Social science as a whole is both intellectually and morally confused. And what is called sociology is very much in the middle of this confusion (Mills 1960:1).

Scientifically insecure and confused, internally diversified and strife-ridden, sociology throughout the last century has struggled continuously with its public image. As a consequence, any idea of *a* public sociology (in the singular) as a magic formula, a sacred incantation or a skeleton key intended to open wide the doors to surrounding society is bound to hit a hard rock and must therefore necessarily be replaced be the idea of public sociolog*ies* (in the plural) that recognizes the plurality of publics sociology may serve but also the plurality of sociologies that the public can seek out. I shall return to this point more substantially later.

MUCH ADO ABOUT PUBLIC SOCIOLOGY

These years, public sociology is the talk of the town, at least in sociology; it is one of the numerous fads of which sociologists with their amnesia and Columbus complexes – constantly believing they have to invent everything from scratch – is famous (see Sorokin 1956). Today, discussions of public sociology have dragged out all the renowned stalwarts of international sociology to comment on and participate in the academic feast as one can see in, for example, the many seminars and conferences on public sociology, the steady stream of books with the term 'public sociology' in their title (like the one before you) and in the symposia on public sociology published by high-ranking social science journals such as *Social Problems*, 51 (1) 2004, *Social Forces*, 82 (4) 2004, *Critical Sociology*, 31 (3) 2005, and *British Journal of Sociology*, 56 (3) 2005. And I bet there is still more, much more, to come which testifies to the fact that at least sociologists take the discussion of public sociology seriously.

Although the idea of public sociology – of *making* sociology public (thereby insinuating that sociology in and by itself is not public) – is as old as the discipline itself, it is not until recently that it as an idea and a concept has captured the sociological imagination of thinkers and practitioners alike. But what is public sociology? Public sociology may, in the succinct definition from Wikipedia, be defined as "an approach to the discipline which seeks to transcend the academy and engage wider audiences. Rather than being defined by a particular method, theory or set of political values, public sociology may be seen as a *style* of sociology, a way of writing and a form of intellectual engagement". The recent appearance of public sociology as such an approach, style or perhaps rather genre or paradigm on the international sociological arena is very much due to the work of one person.

The first to popularize – or perhaps rather revive – the notion of 'public sociology', although the phenomenon and practice of public sociology has existed for almost two centuries, was Michael Burawoy in his presidential address to the American Sociological Association in 2004 and shortly hereafter published in the *American Sociological Review* and other journals (see Burawoy 2004, 2005a, 2005b).[1] After his presentation, public sociology almost immediately became a household – but also a highly contested – concept. But what was his point of departure and his basic ideas? Burawoy believed that contemporary sociologists have given up on the idea of public sociology as practiced by many classical sociologists. For example, he stated that "if our predecessors set out to change the world, we have too often ended up conserving it" (Burawoy 2005a:5). As a consequence, Burawoy detected a growing gap between the sociological ethos and the world sociologists study – something he saw as a cause for serious concern.

In his presidential address, Burawoy – in a similar fashion to Karl Marx's classic response to the ideas of Ludwig Feuerbach – presented eleven theses on the contemporary status of sociology and as a proclamation to colleagues to become more public in orientation. Some of these theses, without recapturing Burawoy's entire argumentation, for example deal with how sociology politically has moved leftward while the rest of the world (Burawoy speaks from a specifically American context)[2] has turned more rightwing, the separation between 'traditional public sociologies' and 'organic public sociologies', the relationship between the individual sociologist's habitus and personal trajectory and the overall development of their discipline, the struggle between and domination of instrumental knowledge over reflexive knowledge, the ascendancy of professional sociology as the apex of sociological knowledge, the particularistic nature of American sociology despite its claims to universalization/globalization, the pressures from and prospects of interdisciplinary knowledge and the sociologist as partisan. All his theses, although I am not sure I can subscribe to all of them, outline a scenario in which sociology has gradually become less public and more internally divided, fragmented and dominated by special interests. Moreover, some of his theses (especially Thesis III and IV) propose an interesting and useful sub-division of sociology into different factions and forms of practice/knowledge. Thus, Burawoy proposed a typology of sociology – a picture of the sociological landscape painted with broad brushstrokes – through which emerge especially four types of sociologies based on the types of audience sociologists are oriented towards and the forms of knowledge they generate. Below a schematic moderation summarizing Burawoy's four sociologies is presented:

Audience Form of knowledge	Academic (internal focus)	Extra-academic (external focus)
Instrumental (focus on means) Knowledge Truth Legitimacy Accountability Politics Pathology	*Professional sociology* (puzzle-solving) Theoretical/empirical Correspondence Scientific norms Peers Professional self-interest Self-referentiality	*Policy sociology* (problem-solving aimed at experts) Concrete Pragmatic Effectiveness Clients Policy intervention Servility
Reflexive (focus on goals/values) Knowledge Truth Legitimacy Accountability Politics Pathology	*Critical sociology* (discussion of values) Foundational Normative Moral vision Critical intellectuals Internal debate Dogmatism	*Public sociology* (dialogical discussion with society on the realization of values) Communicative Consensus Relevance Designated publics Public dialogue Faddishness

Source: Burawoy (2005a:16).

As is evident, all these four types of sociological practice may contain or promote certain pathological seeds or traits whenever they are exaggerated or distorted such as self-referentiality, servility, dogmatism and faddishness. But they may also all serve a genuine purpose, although not all of them seem equally concerned with 'the public. Moreover, when seeing Burawoy's plea for 'public sociology' (the bottom-right box), there is little doubt that he has been inspired by Jürgen Habermas's famous description from the theory of communicative action and his depiction of the ideal society organised as a sociology seminar in which rational minds reach consensus through the persuasion of the better argument and through undistorted dialogue and communication.

Furthermore, Burawoy's model revitalises and reactualises the two classical sociological questions pertaining to 'Knowledge for Whom?' (see Lee 1976) and 'Knowledge for What?' (see Lynd 1939) – two relevant and indeed pertinent questions to ask when talking about the possibilities of public sociology which cannot, however, be separated from the equally important questions of 'Whose Keeper?' (see Wolfe 1989) and 'Knowledge from What?' (see Phillips 1971). All of these questions are of relevance when discussing and seeking to answer questions about what is meant by the public, how can it be reached, why should it be reached and ultimately what is meant by public sociology. Finally, the model also – despite persistent attempts to clarify what is actually meant by 'public sociology' – raises the question: What is a public sociologist? Throughout his numerous papers and presentations, Burawoy himself provides many useful answers and suggestions to this question. However, another sociologist, Herbert J. Gans, hit the nail on the head when, in arguing that more of us should become such 'public sociologists', stated that "a public sociologist is a public intellectual who applies sociological ideas and findings to social (defined broadly) issues about which sociology (also defined broadly) has something to say" (Gans 2002). This is indeed a sympathetic, broad end encompassing conception of public sociology. But does it make us more sensitive to public sociology or any better at performing and practicing public sociology ourselves? I think so – but I also think such programmatic statements should be substantiated and tried out in practice. However, before I reach this conclusion, I will seek briefly to substantiate and problematize any such broad aspirations to describe public sociology while also seeking to steer clear of the danger of monopolizing one way as the only way, the right way of being, doing or thinking public sociology.

Towards Public Sociology

In *The Structural Transformation of the Public Sphere,* Jürgen Habermas (1991) investigated the evolution of the modern bourgeois public sphere and contributed to laying the groundwork for what has later become known as 'public sphere theory'. His description of a specific 'bourgeois public sphere' emerging in the 18th century Europe was particularly aided and abetted by the appearance of critical public discussion fora in coffee houses, the rise of a general reading public and the dissemination of news and information to the public through the press. Historically, the emergence of this bourgeois public sphere coincided with the rise of sociology and most of the classical sociologists – Auguste Comte, Saint-Simon. Karl Marx, Émile Durkheim and Max Weber – were indeed public figures in one way or the other. Some participated in political reform work, others preached a gospel of societal overthrow and revolution, while yet others participated in social work and community improvements. A prominent example of such classical public sociology was Max Weber, who, although vehemently preaching value neutrality, participated in the German peace delegation at the signing of the Treaty of Versailles after World War I. It can hardly be any more public or publicly relevant than this. Today, few if any sociologists are engaged in negotiating peace treaties and few seem to be preoccupied with how to change the world and in what direction. The dangerous and publicly debilitating TINA Syndrome (stating 'There Is No Alternative') has perhaps – after paralyzing and depoliticizing most of the public – now also finally caught up with sociologists (Bauman 2002b). So perhaps the postulated fall of public sociology, as Burawoy laments in his presidential address, can be, and indeed should be, attributed to the simultaneous and more widespread fall of 'public man' in Western societies as such? (Sennett 1977). I will leave the question open for now.

Apart from the TINA Syndrome, many problems, crises and afflictions seem to haunt contemporary sociology (see e.g. Cole 2001).

Some of them pertain to the slow progression of cumulative knowledge in sociology, others revolve around the scientific status of the discipline or the scholarly identity and self-understanding of its practitioners while yet other problems relate to financial funding, political legitimacy or decreasing student intake.[3] These problems, their causes, consequences and scale, naturally vary from country to country and from community to community. Another, and perhaps more global, problem is, as Burawoy suggests, precisely the problematic relationship to the public. Therefore, putting public sociology on the agenda is indeed relevant. As mentioned above, the question remains, however, if *discussing* public sociology overshadows the concern with *practicing* public sociology. Perhaps there is no opposition at all between discussing and doing, one might even surmise. It will be my claim , however, that one could read the rise of the debate on public sociology as a genuine reaction to what Chris Rojek and Bryan S. Turner (2000) memorably termed 'decorative sociology' – the unwanted offspring of the so-called 'cultural turn' in sociology making sociological knowledge aestheticized and politicized but also rather impotent in relation to the public. The consequence of this development, according to Rojek and Turner, has been (1) the rise of a sociology driven by theory and privileging theoretical responsiveness to change, (2) an absence of any commitment to historical or comparative analysis, (3) a fusion of an aestheticized and politicized orientation, and (4) an absence of any tenable, sustained or substantial political agenda (Rojek & Turner 2000:638-639). In their view, decorative sociology, with its concomitant 'ornamentalism', refrains from being public and remains an insulated and secluded activity taking place in academic ivory towers. Rojek and Turner instead argue for an 'engaged detachment' which makes sociology sensitive to the systematic study of reality without lapsing into some sort of self-contained cocoon and which promotes "an attitude to research which recognizes that intellectuals are citizens of societies and therefore have conscious and unconscious attachments to the human formations which they study" (Rojek & Turner 2000:644). According to Rojek and Turner, and I agree with them on this point, the main problem confronting sociology today seems to be that it is too preoccupied with itself while its concern with the public, with the human formations of which sociology is part, is rapidly decreasing.

As I have indicated above, the whole idea of 'public sociology' as advanced from many different quarters of contemporary sociology in recent years may perhaps, and hopefully, prove fruitful and prosperous for the discipline and inspire a public-minded mentality among its practitioners. It may also provide a much-needed bulwark against the spread of so-called inward-looking 'decorative sociology'. But it may also turn into what Burawoy in the model above terms 'faddism' – which may be defined as 'a fashion that is taken up with great enthusiasm for a brief period of time'; something preached rather than practiced, something scholastically stimulating rather than actually carried out, in short ultimately something utterly unpublic or non-public. In fact I do not believe that the idea of public sociology, when it comes down to it, is or should essentially be different from practicing sociology as such, sociology proper. The crucial questions to be asked whenever practicing sociology (and therefore also public sociology) – questions to be asked either by ourselves, by others or by both and which are as time-honoured as the discipline of sociology itself – must be:

(1) What are we doing? (the foundational/vocational question)
(2) How are we doing it? (the technical/operational/methodological question)
(3) Why are we doing it? (the justificational/temperamental question)
(4) Whom are we doing it for? (the directional question)

All these questions, which are closely related to and overlap with the 'Knowledge for What?', 'Knowledge for Whom?', 'Knowledge from What?' and 'Whose Keeper?' questions mentioned above, should and indeed do guide most sociological inquiries. These questions can only be separated from each other analytically – in actual research practice they are inextricably connected – and while some of them may require years of maturation and contemplation for workable answers to appear, others seem to settle in our consciousness much quicker. Although seldom touched upon in conventional sociology or methodology textbooks, the last question – to whom are we aiming to direct our claims to knowledge – is, however, at least as important as the first three and may even end up determining our answering of them. In fact, we will often not be able to answer the first three questions until the fourth has been properly dealt with. This last question can be answered in numerous ways to which I return below. On the overall, however, it can be answered in two fundamentally different ways. First, we are doing sociology for ourselves (the monological/introvert answer). This is, fortunately, a rather seldom response among sociologists. Second, we are doing sociology for others, for somebody else (the dialogical/extrovert answer). The obvious question then arises – who are these others?

THE PUBLICS OF SOCIOLOGY

Sociology may provide knowledge and insight for a variety of publics. So there is a multitude of different publics to or for whom sociologists can write.[4] But 'publics' or the more qualified term 'the public' is indeed a notoriously difficult phenomenon to come to grips with. It seems to evade definition and also raises questions of the existence of the so-called 'general public' but also potential 'counterpublics' (see Warner 2002). One way to try and capture the many publics appealing to sociology, or to whom sociology is itself appealing, would be to take a look at the so-called 'models of relevance' guiding sociological practice. In an illuminating paper,

James B. Rule (1978) enumerated different models of relevance that informed applied as well as purely academic studies. He stated – after conducting an in-depth reading of the history of sociology – how "some sociological writings read as though addressed to potential activists or an aroused public, while others seem intended for a policymaking elite" (Rule 1978:78-79). And indeed, the models of relevance span the entire continuum of potential consumers, recipients, beneficiaries, stakeholders, claims makers and other interested parties. In order to narrow down the field, Rule listed the following five models of relevance oriented towards each their specific section of the public:

1) *No net effects model*: according to this model, the justification of sociology lies in its contribution to enhanced understanding, however without any direct, immediate, intended or observable effects on social life or on the public good. Protagonists will often be concerned with producing knowledge for the sake of knowledge. In short, this is a somewhat conservative model of relevance for sociology.
2) *Direct and positive effects model*: in this model, the main concern is how to benefit as many people as possible – e.g. 'the general public' – and how sociology can assist in ameliorative change, improvement and betterment for society as a whole. In short, this is a rather rationalistic-functionalistic model of relevance for sociology.
3) *Special constituency model – the proletariat*: this model is primarily concerned with enlightening and educating the proletariat into becoming the 'historical subject' in social development and this model therefore specifically sides with the working class in social struggles aimed at destroying the existing (bourgeois/capitalist) social order and in replacing it with a more equal and just substitute. In

short, this is an archetypal Marxist model of relevance for sociology.

4) *Special constituency model – the unco-opted*: this model aims at enhancing the social situation of those at the bottom of society, the underclass, the poor, the deviant and the alienated, racial minorities, those without representation, without resources or without voice. In short, this model is a critical or partisan model of relevance for the marginalized, e.g. progressive action research.

5) *Special constituency model – government officialdom*: this model – according to Rule perhaps the oldest model in sociology – aims at providing knowledge to society (state agencies, authorities or the powers that be) about its citizens, e.g. aiming at increasing information on or control of the population or aimed at improving the livelihood of the inhabitants of a given society. In short, this model is bureaucratic-positivistic.

Obviously, all these models are ideal types difficult to locate in any pure form in real life sociology. Moreover, within each model of relevance certain sub-varieties exist, and some models also overlap considerably. All models of relevance, however, seek to answer the aforementioned questions concerned with whom sociologists write for, whom sociologists regard as their primary constituency and audience and what sociologists think is their social role. In this way, they in each their unique way point out the publics specifically appealing to different varieties of sociology and the sociologies specifically appealing to different varieties of publics.

Another equally illustrative attempt at capturing the public role or function of sociology was proposed by C. Wright Mills. Classically, in *The Sociological Imagination*, he claimed that social scientists, perhaps especially sociologists, can and indeed do perform one of three roles in the field of tension between social science and politics, between science and society, between the world of academia and the public (Mills 1959:179-181). First, the sociologist can be a 'philosopher king'. Executing this role means to claim to know what is good for society as such, why and how to get there and last but not least being able to formulate and attribute this insight to the population at large. Here the sociologist conflates his role as scientist with the role of politician or decision-maker and elevates himself/herself to the esoteric yet powerful position of social umpire. The second – and according to Mills in his lifetime most prominent – role is that of the 'adviser to the king'. Here the sociologist takes a step down the ladder and serves as a provider of knowledge to the powers that be – in Mills's example predominantly as specialized servants in the increasingly rational bureaucratic system. Mills, gloomily, warned particularly against this role, the role as public servant, because

> in this role ... social science itself often tends to become a functionally rational machine; the individual social scientist tends to lose his moral autonomy and the role of reason in human affairs tends to become merely a refinement of techniques for administrative and manipulative uses (Mills 1959:180).

Therefore, and to avoid such colonization of intellectual life by bureaucratic structures, the final role mentioned by Mills is that of the sociologist as a 'public intelligence apparatus'. This means that we, as public sociologists, are expected to

> remain independent, to do one's own work, to select one's own problems, but to direct this work at 'kings' as well as to 'publics'. Such a conception prompts us to imagine social science as a sort of public intelligence apparatus, concerned with public issues and private troubles and with the structural trends of our time underlying them both – and to imagine individual social scientists as rational members of the self-controlled association, which we call the social sciences (Mills 1959:181).

No doubt Mills himself favoured this third role of the social scientist as a public intellectual, the intellectual as a 'craftsman' who through and by his or her work was able to promote social good and change the course of history. This is social science neatly located between autonomy of knowledge and relevancy to publics; it is also social science straddling science and politics. Mills's three examples of public sociology all capture some of the tensions, problems or paradoxes confronting public sociologists – on the one hand how to become socially relevant and of interest to the public (whoever it may be), and on the other how to avoid contamination by external interests (political, bureaucratic or corporate) seeking to control, influence or commission specific scientific results or interpretations. His list can also be used to illustrate a shift in intellectual work from intellectuals, including sociologists, primarily performing the role of philosopher kings or advisors to the king in the early years of social science to the role as parts of a public intelligence apparatus in contemporary society. A similar shift was poignantly described by Zygmunt Bauman (1987) as a shift from intellectuals as 'legislators' in the modern age to intellectuals as 'interpreters' in the postmodern era. Mills's listing above also raises the question whether this is indeed an exhaustive listing of possible public sociologies, and potential publics, when looking at the contemporary social landscape (after all, Mills wrote half a century ago), or whether the status of 'the public' has changed since his time? In order to answer these questions, let me outline four central, and sometimes overlapping, contemporary publics to whom sociological knowledge and insight seem relevant and who in one way or the other often request (or influence) our results, analyses and diagnoses:

1) *Political publics* (e.g. political parties, state agencies, interest groups, etc.).
2) *Commercial publics* (e.g. private stakeholders, the media, corporate companies, etc.).

3) *Educational/academic publics* (e.g. students, academic colleagues, etc.).
4) *Civic publics* (sometimes referred to in the singular as 'the general public', covering a vast and varied field of human actors, agencies and communities as part of everyday life such as, for example, social movements).

Today, all these publics at varying times and varying degrees seem to request sociological knowledge and demand that our results are made available to their specific causes, projects, programmes and interests. What kind of services or end-products is it that these different publics may request or demand from public sociologists? Ragnvald Kalleberg summarised the public relevancy of sociology by looking at where we may find the end-products of sociological/academic work:

1) *Research programmes* resulting in scientific publications.
2) *Teaching and study programmes* resulting in educated students at different levels.
3) *Dissemination programmes* involving the dissemination of ideas resulting in scientific and cultural literacy and contributions to democratic discourse.
4) *'Professional' or expert programmes* resulting in advice or improvement for users/clients.
5) *Self-governance programmes* resulting in well functioning institutions such as university departments, professional associations and academic journals (Kalleberg 2005:388).

Whereas the programmes (1), (2) and (5) primarily cater for what I above labelled educational/academic publics, (3) and (4) can instead be seen as being involved in a variety of publics ranging from political via commercial to civic publics. Although Kalleberg's list is useful for descriptive purposes, it does however seem to privilege sociology's relation to other educational/academic publics on behalf of political, commercial and civic publics. There is, as I see it, an underlying danger that sociology intended merely for other academic audiences or publics becomes introvert, as I shall illustrate below.

However, this proposed proliferation of different publics each requesting different services and different end-products should, *ceteris paribus*, guarantee and secure sociology a high degree of publicity and public demand – it may however, as a side-effect, also ensure that sociologists may easily come to suffer from a 'multiple personality complex', confusion or disorientation, although these would appear to be luxury problems. The main problem, however, often seem to be that sociologists are unable or find it unsuitable to 'sell' themselves to publics – perhaps fearing that they sell out – and this tendency may in turn be reinforced by a lack of public recognition of or attention to what is it is that sociologists are actually good at. A concomitant, and reinforcing, consequence could also be that much sociology may be looked upon by the public as somewhat esoteric and obscure. Thus, in Richard A. Posner's (2001) long list of public intellectuals in a book bearing the same title – a book containing names and descriptions of 550 public intellectuals – only 30 sociologists were included. Moreover, as Herbert J. Gans informs us, another list published by Posner of the top public intellectuals in America, only one sociologist (Alan Wolfe) appeared on the list at a disappointing no. 97. As Gans stated, "the keepers of the 'public intellectual gates' ignore or reject us" (Gans 2002). This either tells us something about sociologists' ability or inability to sell themselves to publics (without simultaneously selling out), something about different public's lack of appreciation of and attention to sociological insights or perhaps something about the combination and reinforced effect of these two unfortunate circumstances (or perhaps it tells us something about how the Posner lists were generated in the first place). And perhaps it is a sin to advertise and sell one's academic knowledge, expertise and ideas to publics. Perhaps it is inappropriate and unbecoming of sociologists to actively seek out or survive on the bread crumbs from the tables of political, commercial or civic publics. Perhaps it is a sell out to produce knowledge that will enhance living or chance the course of the world. The worst sin of all, the original sin, however, is to refrain from contemplating and considering the relevance to publics and turning into an utterly unpublic sociology.

OPPOSING UNPUBLIC SOCIOLOGY

Naturally, it is difficult to be opposed to or position oneself against public sociology. Public sociology sounds nice, it has a positive ring to it and in many ways seems like a pleonasm. However, it may also contain certain oxymoronic features because 'public' may be interpreted or construed in ways that are utterly unpublic. Let me try to qualify this view.

Some of the most heated debates in sociology – from the *Methodenstreit* via the *Werturteilsstreit* to the *Positivismusstreit* – have been about values, biases and political and ideological engagements in social research. One the one side of these disputes protagonists have claimed that "thou shalt not commit a value judgment" (Gouldner 1962:199), whereas on the other we find those who think sociology can be – or cannot avoid being – a useful platform for value-oriented or political sympathies. As Howard S. Becker, for example, once stated on the political ideals and ideological sympathies of many sociologists – something that has not changed considerably despite almost half a decade has passed:

> It is no secret that most sociologists are politically liberal to one degree or another. Our political preferences dictate the side we will be on and, since those preferences are shared by most of our colleagues, few are ready to throw the first stone or are even aware that stone-throwing is a possibility. We usually take the side of the underdog; we are for Negroes and against Fascists. We do not think anyone biased who does research designed to

> prove that the former are not as bad as people think or that the latter are worse (Becker 1967:244).

Although I find it difficult to disagree that we are and indeed should be, almost per definition, "for Negroes and against Fascists", I also think it may prove extremely dangerous if sociology *as a scientific discipline* (and here I am not thinking of the preferences of individual sociologists as such) takes sides or becomes synonymous with a particular political stance, cause or idea. This may prove perilous to our public image as publicly responsible sociologists. Therefore, public sociology needs to steer clear of the Scylla of ideological or political roles on the one side and of the Charybdis of disengaged and clinical roles on the other. This may indeed be a matter of walking a tight robe, and it sometimes happens that sociologists – individually or collectively – fall too heavily on one side – quite often, in Becker's description above, they tend to fall on the same side. To provide an example, John Holmwood (2005) informs us how the American Sociological Association passed a motion in 2003 against the Iraq War in which the vast majority of sociologists voted against American military intervention. Although the motion did not have any impact on the overall course of American politics, I believe it would be utterly unthinkable – and also utterly unacceptable – if Dansk Sociologforening (the Danish Sociological Association) would ever engage its members in passing motions or voting proceedings regarding such highly politicized issues. And this, I think, is how it should be. Sociology as public social science can and should concern itself with what 'is' and what 'could be' but it should not try to dictate what 'should be'. Then it would not be public sociology but politicized sociology. Sociology is not a matter of opinion (not even public opinion) – it is, and remains, a matter of knowledge. Therefore, in my view it is neither more noble nor less particularistic to support specific political causes, no matter how sympathetic or worthy, as a practicing sociologist or in the name of sociology than it is to lend one's abilities, faculties and claims to knowledge to a specific profit-oriented private organization or company. In either case, the public is transformed into a particularistic public and sociology into a discipline that loses scientific autonomy and public credibility.

Perhaps no one succeeded better in advocating the public agenda of sociology as a combined publicly engaged and yet scientifically sound, autonomous and credible discipline than Pierre Bourdieu. As Bourdieu, a sociologist who throughout his own lifetime gradually turned ever more public (some would even say political) and underwent nothing less than a personal metamorphosis, as it were, from the early years' parading as a 'sociologists' sociologist' to a publicly intervening sociologist in his later years – remarked in the preface to his controversial book *Contre-feux 2*; a book that was perhaps also 'for burning', as he himself described one of his earlier book:

> I run the risk of shocking those [researchers] who, opting for the cozy virtuousness of confinement within their ivory tower, see intervention outside the academic sphere as a dangerous failing of that famous 'axiological neutrality' this is wrongly equated with scientific objectivity ... But I am convinced that we must at all costs bring the achievements of science and scholarship into public debate, from which they are tragically absent (Bourdieu quoted in Poupeau & Discepolo 2004:76).

Bourdieu – especially in his later years – argued for such an engaged, committed and public sociology that remains scientifically valid and abides by the criteria of scientific reasoning and documentation without lapsing into positivistic ideas of 'axiological neutrality', objectivity and social detachment. Any public sociology worthy of its name, I believe, should exactly be able to balance engaged relevance to the public with conventional scientific criteria separating science from non-science or pseudo-science.

In order to define what is public about the public sociology I envision and wish to promote in this introductory chapter, the best way is perhaps to point out the tendency for the opposite – unpublic or what I call 'introvert' sociology. Introvert or unpublic sociology can be found many different places, among many different practitioners and comes in many different guises and I here offer merely four types that are, indeed, caricatures, although most of us would know at least a colleague or two whose work fits very well into one of these categories: (1) *ivory tower sociology* thriving on providing elevated and esoteric interpretations of social life from afar, without any real life contact or research results, as performed for example by those Walter Korpi (1990) labelled the 'pegasi' of sociology; (2) *peer review sociology* concerned with keeping the engine of sociology as career smoothly running by a constant outpouring of specialized articles in journals on topics of little or no public interest; (3) *conference sociology* wonderfully depicted by David Lodge's novel *Small World* – an intellectual life lived on airplanes, in lecture theatres and conference halls and at academic soirees around the world with no bearing on the lives of other people than the conference participants themselves; and finally (4) *politicized sociology* which mistakes public engagement and commitment with ideological outbursts and political sympathies and which regards itself as the moral mouthpiece for specific political causes or programmes. Many would perhaps count politicized sociology among very extrovert variants of the discipline – to me, however, politicized sociology is often concerned more with expounding and exposing the 'right' ideas and opinions, thereby legitimating itself, than with providing relevant analyses or useful answers to pressing social problems. In all cases, the ideas and interpretations of such unpublic or introvert sociology seldom reach beyond the rituals of academic regurgitation and recitation or beyond the threshold of confined and stuffy back rooms of particularistic political movements. So where the latter politicized form of sociology suffers from equating the political with the scientific, the former three hardly recognize anything outside the world of the academy – they symbolize what Ian Shapiro recently termed the "flight from reality in the human sciences (Shapiro 2005). On this paradoxical form of introversion, of sociology turning its back on the real world and simultaneously turning itself into its own public, Philip Davies succinctly wrote:

> [A] problem with some sociologists is that they often communicate with each other in a language that is opaque, impenetrable and inaccessible ... Sociology seems to have become inward looking, tribal and inaccessible. The so-called scientific value of sociology often appears to have an inverse relationship to its utility. Many research projects undertaken by sociologists ask questions that are of interest to nobody other than fellow sociologists ... Moreover, many sociologists, in common with other disciplines and professions, lack the communication skills to reach those who are struggling to find solutions to pressing problems ... The debates that take place in many sociological journals are of little or no relevance to analysts or policy makers ... Indeed, they often have little or no relevance to anyone other than professional sociologists (Davis 2004:449; see also Jacobsen 2006a on this tendency).

Quite a few of these introverted sociologists – ivory tower, peer review, conference and politicized sociologists – would probably suffer from septic shock if forced focus on reality, if forced to become real public sociologists, sociologists with a *real* interest in the public. One is safe as long as nobody knows or understands what one is doing, seems to be the strategy guiding many introverts practicing ivory tower, peer review or conference sociology, whereas the strategy guiding many politicized sociologists seems to be that one is safe as long as one uncritically supports the, almost per definition, 'good causes', or as long as one is capable of stating that everybody else is in the wrong, wear blinkers or have misinterpreted or misunderstood the 'real' nature of the problem.[5]

This critique aimed at certain varieties of introverted sociology mirrors and buttresses the critique of critical and professional as advanced also by Michael Burawoy (2005a) for being publicly inaccessible and incomprehensible and for being primarily concerned with the world of the academy. Thus, because I – like Burawoy – believe in public sociology, public sociology should be public in the sense of taking an interest in what is termed 'the general public' (what I above called 'civic publics') and less interested in believing itself to be a protagonist or standard-bearer of specific publics – political, commercial, educational/academic or otherwise. As Herbert J. Gans contended in his plea that more of us should indeed become public sociologists, "scientists' taboos against addressing the general public must be overcome" (Gans 2002). This naturally raises the intricate questions of: Does 'the general public' exist any more? Did it ever? What does it look like? Although highly relevant, these questions cannot be answered in this specific context. I do believe, however, that an approximation to what counts as 'the general public' is indeed possible – it is a public whose private troubles and public issues are commonly and routinely experienced by many or most parts of the population at large.[6] And it is indeed also possible to conduct sociological research that appears to be relevant to the general public. For example, in their groundbreaking *Habits of the Heart*, Robert N. Bellah and colleagues called for social science turning into 'public philosophy' – a sociology according to them concerned with 'the whole of society' – a social science which, they claimed, could not be entirely value free, which had to avoid excessive specialization and narrow professionalization, which must attempt to open up to and break down the iron curtain separating it from scholars within the humanities as well as philosophers and social historians, which must look at values as much as at facts, and which must be critical and dialogical. They wrote of this idea of sociology as public philosophy:

> Social science as public philosophy is public not just in the sense that its findings are publicly available or useful to some group or institution outside the scholarly world. It is public in that it seeks to engage the public in dialogue. It also seeks to engage the 'community of the competent', the spe-

cialists and the experts, in dialogue, but it does not seek to stay within the boundaries of the specialist community while studying the rest of society from outside ... Without a public, social science as public philosophy will wither away (Bellah, Madsen, Sullivan, Swidler & Tipton 1985/1996:303).

Such programmatic statements are, obviously, important and welcome because they point to notions and ideas of how sociology may become publicly relevant and useful. What is more important however – something that *Habits of the Heart* also proved – is that it is indeed possible to reach the vast reading public, 'the general public', the millions of citizens out there with a book containing a sober sociological analysis of society. To date the book has been, and continues to be, one of the most welcome bestseller within sociology. This shows how public sociology can be preached, but most important of all how it needs to be practiced.

Thus, because I – like Michael Burawoy and many others – believe in public sociology (but contrary to Burawoy remain adamantly opposed to politicized sociology), I also allow myself to be critical of certain types of publicly engaged sociologies. Sociology cannot only become *too introvert*, as the above suggested; it can also become *too extrovert*. Let me provide one illustrative example. On the other hand – although I am in favour of the recent much publicized and debated transition from *Mode I* social science (the introverts) to *Mode II* social science (the more extroverted) changing the demands on and directions of also sociology (see Gibbons et al. 1994; Nowotny et al. 2001; Stokes 1997) – I think it dangerous if commercial publics or media publics are successful in setting or colonizing the agenda for ever-increasing sections of social research. There is, perhaps especially in these years of declining public and government funding for social research and an increased focus on 'publish or perish' and media performances among academics, a danger of the privatization of publics – that 'the general public' of sociology becomes synonymous with big corporate businesses, commercial enterprises, privately owned research funds or media audiences with an insatiable appetite for messenger boys, easily digestible entertainment and slapstick sociology. Thus, becoming excessively extroverted – i.e. allowing commercial interests or media moguls to dictate or shape the content of social research – is equally dangerous to becoming increasingly introverted. As Buravoy explains: "The interest in a public sociology is, in part, a reaction to the privatization of everything" (Burawoy 2005a:7). Public sociology can thus be seen as a reaction to the privatization of society, and possibly also the potential for a privatization of sociology.

Not everybody, however, have been equally positive in their reception of especially Michael Burawoy's idea of public sociology and quite a few sociologists have been either moderately appreciative or overtly critical of his by now much publicized understanding of public sociology. John Holmwood, for one, opposed what he believed to be Burawoy's position: that public sociology is a partisan/political project. To Holmwood, political neutrality is central to the corporate organization of sociology unless sociology is to be conflated with politics (Holmwood 2007). According to Charles R. Tittle (2004), Burawoy's idea of public sociology is deemed arrogant and would therefore be a grave mistake if institutionalized because it involves false assumptions about the moral or social superiority of sociology; it endangers what little legitimacy sociology has been able to achieve; it is incompatible with good professional sociology; and it is at odds with the idea of equal participation of all citizens because it paradoxically ends up privileging sociological insights. Finally, Mathieu Deflem, in a very harsh and uncompromising critique of Burawoy, stated that his idea of public sociology is

> neither public nor sociology. Public sociology is not a plea to make sociology more relevant to the many publics in society nor to connect sociology democratically to political activity. Of course, sociologists should be public intellectuals. But they should be and can only be public intellectuals as practitioners of the science they practice, not as activists left or right. Yet, public sociology instead is a quest to subsume sociology under politics, a

politics of a specific kind, not in order to foster sociological activism but to narrow down the sociological discipline to activist sociology. That this activism is predominantly leftist in orientation is residual to the broader issue of the true agenda of public sociology (Mathieu 2004).

According to Mathieu, Burawoy reveals himself as a spokesman (indeed a Marxist spokesman) in favour of sociology becoming politically engaged and activist. I agree with Mathieu that this indeed a dangerous development, but I do not and cannot see Burawoy's plea for public sociology as a justification of Marxist social science, although there are certain unambiguous sympathies for politicized sociology. However, I will not comment more substantially on these points of criticism raised against Burawoy's position here but I merely want to illustrate that the idea of public sociology is far from uncontroversial and that the danger of sociology – indeed also as public sociology – becoming unpublic is ever-present.

From Double to Triple Hermeneutic

Not so long ago, Zygmunt Bauman observed on contemporary liquid modern society, in which intellectual knowledge along everything else becomes a commodity and part of the consumerist syndrome, how "it seems that the world prefers to honour its philosophers by memorial plaques than by listening to them, let alone by following their advice" (Bauman 2002:108). This is indeed an accurate description of the fate of much intellectual and scholarly work (including sociological) today – that it, like all other items and goods, is uncritically consumed in order to satisfy immediate desires and demands and that it leaves no further traces or permanent imprint on the running of the world. There is, however, a fate worse than this – the fate of sociology becoming indifferent to publics and the public becoming disinterested in sociology and disinclined to learn from sociological insight.

Above I have discussed, at times in a consciously chosen polemical tone, the background for the current debate on public sociology. I have also discussed some of the content of and the various positions (and shown some more unpublic than others) within the debate and gradually moved towards my own position of what may be a broad and encompassing understanding of public sociology. My main ambition has been the avoidance of 'public sociology' itself becoming a scholastic paradigm or unworldly preoccupation – something talked about in academic circles rather than carried out, an academic specialty rather than a steppingstone to make the academic relevant. My answer is therefore neither very sophisticated nor perhaps very original. I merely want to argue for what I wish to term a 'triple hermeneutic' as a template for conducting public sociology – now and in the future. Whereas conventional philosophical hermeneutics, the theory of interpretation, has almost exclusively privileged the interpreter (i.e. the philosopher, sociologist or intellectual) as the one 'in the know' on behalf of those interpreted, the triple hermeneutic rather privilege *the relation* between interpreter and interpreted. No one takes priority over the other and each are as interested in and inspired by the insights and ideas stemming from the other party in the relationship as the other.

Some years ago, a tiny step towards a triple hermeneutic was proposed – a step which, however, only took us halfway. Anthony Giddens famously insisted that sociology and surrounding society are mutually involved in a so-called 'double hermeneutic'. He defined this double hermeneutic in the following fashion:

> Sociology ... deals with a universe which is already constituted within frames of meaning by social actors themselves, and reinterprets these within its own theoretical schemes, mediating ordinary and technical language. This double hermeneutic is of considerable complexity, since the connection is not merely a one-way one ... There is a continual 'slippage' of the concepts constructed in sociology, whereby these are appropriated

by those whose conduct they were originally coined to analyse, and hence tend to become integral features of that conduct (Giddens 1976:162).

In Giddens's understanding, there is a continuous and apparently equal exchange between sociology and society whereby the realm of social life and the realm of academic contemplation and social research mutually and in frictionless fashion influence each other. Thus, according to his perspective, "sociological knowledge spirals in and out of the universe of social life, reconstructing both itself and that universe as an integral part of that process" (Giddens 1990:15-16). I do not disagree with this proposed description of the double hermeneutic relationship between sociology and society – I do believe, however, that Giddens's position needs some clarification and expansion because it seems to start from nowhere – it seems to provide a classic example of the chicken or the egg riddle; either social life or sociology comes first but we cannot really decide. Moreover, it seems as if Giddens takes the existence and practice of this 'double hermeneutic' for granted – it *is* just there. This requires two comments. First, Giddens's double hermeneutic postulates some sort of *unio mystico* between sociology and surrounding society (i.e. the general public). My objection to this view is that he seems to think that, from the outset, we have people in everyday life, thinking, acting and relating. Then along comes the ingenious sociologist and interprets what they think and do and how they relate. Finally, this means that people – because they are reflexive and knowledgeable – will automatically accept and actually use sociological insights in their everyday endeavours and sociologists will simultaneously learn something new from their contacts with people, something which they also automatically will incorporate into their sophisticated models and theories. What happens in the process of the double hermeneutic, however, seems utterly magic. Nowhere does Giddens elaborate on whether people will *actually* take sociologists and their theories, concepts and analyses seriously or whether sociologists will *actually* be sensitive to and interested in what people do. According to the triple hermeneutic, society and sociology *are* already constituted (as an ontological premise), so there is no chicken and egg riddle, but if sociology is to be of relevance to society, it needs to start looking at itself first. It cannot expect society to save sociology (or sociology to save society) – sociology, in other words, needs to begin by looking at itself. My second objection is that Giddens seems to think that the public, willy-nilly and almost uncritically, will embrace, care about and take an active interest in what sociologists do or say. To me, a triple hermeneutic is something to be worked on actively and continuously; it is about sociology making itself valuable to the public; it is about the public hopefully reaching out to sociology and sociology at the same time reaching out to the public. There is a threefold process involved here, hence a *triple* hermeneutic. First, sociologists interpret a world that people themselves have already interpreted in advance (Giddens's position). Then sociologists interpret and analyse this world and in various forms and through various channels send their results back to people (Giddens is till with me on this). Finally, as the third step, the public may subsequently accept or reject the insights provided by sociologist in their daily doings and organization of society (on this Giddens is either quiet or takes it for granted). It is exactly in this final step that public sociology is needed – sociology cut to the measure of what the general public finds useful or may request. Today, perhaps more than ever before, sociology finds itself in a cutthroat competitive situation with other scientific disciplines or agencies willing to cater for the demands and interests of people, the general public. Sociology therefore needs to take a long and hard look at itself and find out what it is that it can specifically provide that other suppliers are incapable of or unsuited for. This is not a matter of selling out or becoming a commodity for uncritical consumption – it is a matter of taking the public seriously if the public should take sociology seriously.

The triple hermeneutic advocated and presented here merely in sketchy form – and which requires more systematic formulation and substantiated refinement – may be described in the following tentative way: *The triple hermeneutic is concerned with how sociology may be of use to and relevance for the general public. It takes as its starting point a deep-seated sociological curiosity about the lives and concerns of people. It ceaselessly asks what sociology can do for the general public rather than what the general public can do for sociology. It is, perhaps shamelessly, concerned with the multitude of private troubles and public issues that flourish within different general publics in all human societies. Moreover, it is not suspicious of scholars and researchers who take a genuine and unreserved interest in what is going on in the real world. Therefore, it ceaselessly compiles information and data from reality which materialize in sociological analyses, diagnoses and interpretations, some descriptive, others critical. Subsequently, these analyses, diagnoses and interpretations are once again – either in written, oral or mediated form – directed to and distributed among the general public in a form understandable to most ordinary people who may decide to use the newly gained insight to do things differently, if they wish. However, there are no guarantees whatsoever that the general public will care about sociology, but sociology will continue to care about the general public. And the premise is that the general public will only care about sociology because sociology cares about the general public. Finally, the triple hermeneutic insists that sociologists refrain from taking sides in questions pertaining to politics and equally politically pertinent issues of the day – sociology is expected to provide sober analyses, diagnoses or interpretations to the general public that comply with the standards of scientific inquiry but which, at the same time, may potentially provide knowledge to general publics about how, why and in which situations to do things differently.* To summarize, contrary to or perhaps rather as an extension of the double hermeneutic, the triple hermeneutic claims that sociology must start with itself and its relation to the outside world. This means that sociology takes the world seriously by accepting that there is or must be a demand, latent of manifest, for sociological knowledge. It also means that publics may chose to ignore or even withdraw support of sociology, if sociology fails to deliver analyses, diagnoses or interpretations deemed valuable by the general public. The overall aim is to expand or transform the philosophically oriented 'hermeneutic circle' (conventionally understood as an interpretive process in which part and whole mutually interact with and shape each other, thereby enhancing understanding) with a 'hermeneutic spiral' or, perhaps more poetically visual, a 'hermeneutic drill' which is not content merely with rotating but which, when placed against a solid brick-wall, will work its way deep into and alter the very texture of what we call society. Without such a triple hermeneutic with its open-ended sociological dialogue with and drilling into the world of the public, we may end up with sociological introversion and self-containment of which Zygmunt Bauman poignantly stated:

> If what sociology does does not matter, it can do whatever it likes. This is a tempting possibility: to immerse oneself fully in one's own specialized discourse inside which one feels comfortably at home, to savour the subtleties of distinction and discretion such discourse demands and renders possible, to take the very disinterestedness of one's pursuits for the sign of their supreme value, to take pride in keeping alive, against the odds, a precious endeavour for which the rest, the polluted or corrupted part of the world, has (temporarily, one would add, seeking the comfort of hope) no use (Bauman 1992:106-107).

To conduct research in the interest of the public or to provide research-based feedback to the public, however, does far from entail that the researcher is currying favours with the public, e.g. interest groups, funding agencies or state authorities. It entails a role for the researcher as installing a critical mentality among the recipients or users of the knowledge he or she provides. As Emma Clare correctly observed: "This is not just in the sense of reporting issues in a way that your audience can easily understand and make use of, where relevant. It is also about reporting issues in a way that will make the audience potentially more receptive to the issues" (Clare in Rappert 1999:708). Understanding and illuminating are, however, not always identical processes and the purpose of the triple hermeneutic is exactly to secure that understanding and illumination are mutually inspired. Therefore, sociology as a triple hermeneutic public enterprise needs and seeks to achieve two things at the same time – to make the unfamiliar world of people familiar to them (*refamiliarization*), while also making the familiar world of people unfamiliar to them (*defamiliarization*). Whereas the former tries to make the world comprehensible and safe to its inhabitants, so that they may go about their daily doings without worrying and feeling vulnerable, the latter demands of them never to take the world they encounter for granted or to allow themselves be lulled into believing that it cannot be different. So if we are to understand and appreciate public sociology as a triple hermeneutic, as I have suggested above, *it is not merely about getting sociology interested in the public; it is also about getting the public interested in sociology.* Thus, according to Michael Burawoy, public sociology (practiced as what he calls a 'triple dialogue' not very different from my 'triple hermeneutic') is primarily about leaving the ivory towers of intellectual and academic seclusion and move out into the real world of real people and real problems:

> It is [about] taking sociology to publics beyond the university, engaging them in dialogue about public issues that have been studied by sociologists. Indeed it is a triple dialogue – a dialogue among sociologists, between sociologists and most importantly within publics themselves (Burawoy 2005c:71).

I also believe Burawoy captured it very well when, in his personal statements in connection to the American Sociological Association elections, clarified on the content of public sociology:

> As mirror and conscience of society, sociology must define, promote and inform public debate about deepening class and racial

inequalities, new gender regimes, environmental degradation, market fundamentalism, state and non-state violence. I believe that the world needs public sociology – a sociology that transcends the academy – more than ever. Our potential publics are multiple, ranging from media audiences to policy makers, from silenced minorities to social movements. They are local, global and national. As public sociology stimulates debate in all these contexts, it inspires and revitalizes our discipline. In return, theory and research give legitimacy, direction and substance to public sociology. Teaching is equally central to public sociology: students are our first public for they carry sociology into all walks of life. Finally, the critical imagination, exposing the gap between what is and what could be, infuses values into public sociology to remind us that the world could be different (see 'public sociology' at Wikipedia.org).

Thus, there is, and must be, a certain utopian element or potential involved in public sociology – the world could and perhaps even should be a better place to live, but according to the triple hermeneutic it is not up to the sociologist to decide or define it. Sociology may provide knowledge to the general public about what is and what could be done about the world – sociology, however, should not be presumptuous enough to tell the public what should be done about it. The positive effect of sociology is therefore not to be found in pointing out destinations to be reached but in proposing different routes open to be tried out. Likewise, Herbert J. Gans stated on the potentially positive social effects of public sociology:

> Public sociology of all kinds is badly needed. It can demonstrate that sociology adds distinctive insights and findings; increase the discipline's relevance by forcing it to analyze current events and issues; and enhance sociology's visibility. More important, public sociology is a way of telling the general public what we do and how we are spending public money. If we do it well, public sociology may help to attract more and better students, increase research funds and earn us public support when sociology

is under attack from hostile ideological and political organizations. Perhaps someday, public sociologists will even be properly represented among the 100 most visible public intellectuals (Gans 2002).

Not that the end-goal of practising public sociology in itself is to appear on a list of the most visible public intellectuals, but it might somewhat prove to the general public that we do, in fact, have something interesting and important to say. Finally, I wish to warn against the imminent danger of 'public sociology' becoming unpublic or non-public. If we are not cautious, public sociology is itself in jeopardy of turning into something like *professional sociology*, *peer review sociology* or the like, in which it becomes a popular fad, a token of academic introversion or a self-perpetuating paradigm talking to itself about itself. We therefore need to be wary that public sociology moves beyond discussions of 'public sociology' within the confines of sociology and proves its worth in real life. This reminds me of Harold Garfinkel's classic contention that sociologists are like goldfish swimming in a bowl, confidently analyzing other goldfish, without having ever stopped to recognize the bowl and the water they have in common with the fish they study. What we need to do is to realize that our discipline is thoroughly dependent on the fact that the other fish keep swimming, and that the destiny of our discipline is inextricably connected to these other fish swimming in the water.

THE BACKGROUND FOR AND STRUCTURE OF THE BOOK

As pointed out above by Michael Burawoy, public sociology is not merely about researching, it is also about teaching since students are "our first public for they carry sociology into all walks of life", as he insisted. This book celebrates the decennary anniversary of the Sociology Program at Aalborg University, which is a combined research and teaching program. The Sociology Program has throughout its ten years continuously insisted on providing students with a teaching environment in which practical skills are intimately combined with theoretical knowledge. This means that the students, as well as the teachers involved, are all engaged in finding out how their theoretical ideas may be put into practice as well as how practical engagements with or interventions into social reality and parts of the public requires a modicum of theoretical ballast. This is primarily achieved by privileging no theoretical schools of thought, no methodological doctrines and no methods of social research over others. Such an open environment has persistently inspired students, and scholars, to carry out creative research and to conduct investigations of a variety of topics, themes and subject matters of high academic quality. According to one of the prime movers of the Sociology Program, the intentions were to create the foundations for what was called a 'vedkommende sociologi' (a Danish term capturing and reflecting both the idea of *relevancy* and *applicability*). Such a 'vedkommende sociologi' is also *an embedded sociology* (embedded in the classical tradition of sociology but always willing to ask new and relevant questions pertaining to the problems confronting contemporary society), *a critical sociology* (willing to wrestle with authorities and ask sometimes annoying and provocative questions), and finally *an extrovert sociology* (in which engagement in and with the world and its publics takes precedence over the worship of method, theory or the discipline in and by itself)(Tonboe 2003). Moreover, the Sociology Program has always prided itself – and for good reason – of educating coming generations of sociologists with a public profile stemming from a problem-based learning strategy, project-work organization and group-work as the pedagogical and scholarly backbones. This public profile can, amongst other places, be detected in the Program's continuous preoccupation with and focus on student internship, research-based teaching and teaching-based research. In all cases, the students at Aalborg are requested and challenged to thinking publicly. In short, the Sociology Program has continuously aimed at educating future generations of sociologists for whom contact with and interest in the general public is part and parcel of their natural attitude and their self-conception as sociologists. They have been trained in the understanding – as advanced by Zygmunt Bauman, echoing Jürgen Habermas, at the inaugural conference of the Sociology Program in 1997 entitled *The Sociology of the Future* – that "good sociology, like a good social worker, wishes to work itself out of its job" (Bauman 1998:48). And true, sociologists trained at and translocated from Aalborg University are inspired to think of themselves and their practice as relevant to the private troubles, public issues and social problems of surrounding society.

The conference celebrating the ten years anniversary was entitled *Public Sociology* and took place in October 2007 and in many respects the concerns and discussions from the aforementioned inaugural conference, *The Sociology of the Future*, then came full-circle. This does not mean, however, that any definitive or authoritative solutions were offered to the intricate relationship between sociology and the public, but many fruitful suggestions were advanced by keynote speakers as well as by other invited presenters. As such, the relationship between sociology and the public is an ongoing and never-ending aspect of doing and thinking sociology. All the chapters included in this book have been reworked from oral presentations delivered at the anniversary conference as invited keynote speakers were asked to contribute with chapters for this book of proceedings and thereby put their words into writing. All the contributors were asked to think about and comment on their own relation to their discipline from the perspective of public sociology. To all of them, they later revealed, this was indeed a somewhat daunting task although all contributors for years have thought hard, struggled with and written about, implicitly or explicitly, the prospects for and obstacles to a public sociology. These thoughts and thought-provoking ideas are illustrated in their respective chapters to follow this introduction.

In Chapter 1 by *Ottar Brox*, we encounter the discussion, also entertained by Michael Burawoy in his writings on public sociology, of the possible disappearance of public sociology from the face of the earth. Brox, himself a lifelong champion and practitioner of public/political sociology in Norway, writes from the perspective of someone who has been able to observe how sociology has changed throughout the latter part of the 20th century. He states, however, that "if you expect nostalgic laments with the message that everything, including sociology, was better half a century ago, you will be disappointed". He does, however, admit that despite many improvements in methodology and theory throughout the years, much of contemporary sociology lacks the type of engagement with the public that was a hallmark of much of the sociology carried out by Brow himself and others in their studies of for example northern Norwegian fringe communities in the 1960s. He states that "the general public has a legitimate interest in our work, just like professional colleagues and the authorities or organizations which finance our projects". Therefore, sociology needs to take the public seriously. Brox's ambition is therefore to make sociology a 'solvent of doxa' (Loïc Wacquant's term) whereby he means that sociology as a public discipline needs to counter, criticise and dissolve common sense. Brox then applies this notion of 'solvent of doxa' to debates of a political and economic character in contemporary Norway and how sociology may contribute with valuable insights and ideas. Brox's clarion call to sociologists is urging them to "let the prospects for controversies trigger our *professional curiosity*, as we are more likely to produce interesting and useful knowledge by getting involved in controversies than looking for more or less plausible, but usually also more or less ineffective arguments for good causes". As such, a public sociology is a *publicly engaged* sociology.

Chapter 2 by *Bent Flyvbjerg* discusses the possibilities of taking sociology beyond epistemological (*episteme*) and technological (*techne*) practices and into the realm of *phronesis* – the value-oriented discussion of where we are heading as society. Thus, phronesis is an academic virtue that pays heed to the public concerns and practical challenges confronting this society. Flyvbjerg, a local scholar with a global outlook, believes that public sociology as such phronetic sociology needs to rid itself of any illusions of emulating the natural sciences, that it must address problems that matter to groups in the local, national and global communities in which we live, that it must do it in ways that matter, and that it should effectively and dialogically communicate the results of sociological research to fellow citizens, the 'public', and carefully listen to their feedback. This view of social science, and its reception among colleagues around the world, has recently been described as the 'Flyvbjerg effect' (Schram & Caterino 2006). Throughout the chapter, Flyvbjerg initially differentiates phronetic sociology from other types of sociology or social thought by tracing its roots to ancient Greek philosophy, by illustrating its perspective on comprehending, approaching and researching reality (i.e. through the priority of the particular, the focus on power, the concern with values, the desire to get close to reality, the preoccupation with practice before discourse, the intensive focus on little things, the concern with cases and contexts, the focus on the 'how' of social practice, the ambition to bridge agency and structure and the engaging in a continuous dialogue with a polyphony of voices). Subsequently, Flyvbjerg shows – from a selection of actual studies – examples of how such phronetic sociology may be practiced and on which particular topics. He writes that the ambition of phronetic sociology is, in short, to "find avenues to praxis" and to "outline how things could be done differently". This may only be achieved, and be of relevance, if the knowledge provided by sociology recognizes that "we cannot find ultimate answers to these questions or even to a single version of what the questions are". A phronetic public sociology, as Flyvbjerg shows, is thus an endlessly inquisitive endeavour.

James B. Rule, in Chapter 3, deals with sociology's relationship with and relevance to the wider public, broadly understood. Rule starts out with a provocative question: "Imagine that our discipline was miraculously eliminated – wiped off the intellectual map, with departments disbanded, degrees expunged, learned associations somehow mysteriously vaporized. Would anyone notice the loss ... or feel the need to redress it?". The question is rhetorical – and so is the answer. As mentioned above, Rule already many years ago invented the valuable and illustrative concept of 'models of relevance' and he applies this concept to the current status and situation of sociology. Like Flyvbjerg in the previous chapter, Rule is also sceptical of adopting the previously prominent natural scientific view as an ideal for sociology because it does not necessarily entail an orientation towards the public. According to him, all sociologists will be motivated by some sort of model of relevance in their work – as a point of departure and as a destination. Such models of relevance are "accounts of how the understanding generated by our work actually moves specific intellectual 'consumers', and how such consumption contributes to making the world a better place". Thus, all models of relevance, Rule instructs us, are oriented towards the betterment of the conditions of a certain type of public or aimed at providing knowledge for a certain sector of society. In his chapter, Rule discusses the background and current status of some of the so-called 'master models of relevance' such as those proposed by Karl Marx, Herbert Spencer, Émile Durkheim or C. Wright Mills. Where do they stand today? Rule's answer is rather gloomy – there has been a relentless dismantling of or decline in such master models or grand narratives in contemporary society. He writes: "Working sociologists simply seem much less likely to perceive themselves as joining broad categories of other researchers in a single, master process of ameliorative social change". The reasons are as many as are the consequences. Sociologists have lost the collective interest in contemplating a different, and indeed better, future and with it also lost a substantial proportion of and propensity to public relevance. Today, there is no longer one dominant model of relevance – there exists a multitude unlikely ever to coagulate into one single vision – for better and for worse.

In Chapter 4 by *Henrik Dahl* we encounter an opposition between 'pure/academic' sociology on the one hand and 'applied/practical' social research on the other. Dahl, himself managing and working in a private consultant and research company, is critical of the former type of sociology. He is not opposed to pure sociology as such but wonders about certain aspects often associated with the work of pure sociologists, e.g., "the frequent lack of social graces among those who study the social; the aggression towards deviant colleagues – even among the champions of tolerance in the general society, and the way care for the lot of the ordinary citizen is usually expressed in language and concepts entirely un-intelligible by the common man". Dahl's position is that applied social research – research aimed at providing recommendations or even solutions to actual social problems – is a much more precarious but in many respects also a much more rewarding enterprise than purely speculating on or theoretically interpreting social reality. Thus, throughout the chapter Dahl compares and contrasts pure to practical sociology by claiming that "being a practical academic raises questions of risk and responsibility … which are very different from the problems the pure academic has to deal with". These risks and responsibilities to a large degree concern contact with the public such as organizations or companies commissioning or requesting sociological analyses. In fact, quite a lot of the work carried out under the auspices of pure sociology never reaches the public. As Dahl asserts, "there is no general population anxiously waiting for pure sociologists to bring release from pain or premature death". Metaphysical uncertainty coupled with a lack of pragmatic application makes pure sociology a poor champion of public sociology. Therefore, Dahl proposed that pure sociology – if it is to be of any relevance to other parties than itself – needs to return to common standards of criticism and relevancy also found elsewhere in the scientific community.

Chapter 5 by *Keith Tester* locates the debate on public sociology within the realm of contemporary media landscape. Like Dahl before him, Tester contrasts 'public sociology' to what he labels 'private sociology' and writes: "There can be a *public* sociology only to the extent that it is possible for sociology to appear before audiences that are not exclusively constituted by a professional group that defines itself in terms of the occupation of the institutions and channels of communication of an academic discipline". Private sociology – sociology solely aimed at other sociologists (what I above called 'introvert sociology') – is not and cannot become public because it does not seek to occur before any non-academic audiences. One of the major channels of communication for sociology concerned with reaching beyond such purely academic audiences, Tester claims, is through the media. But also the media – or the 'media environment' – has its own ways of dealing with sociological insights (e.g. through domination and distortion) because the media are part and parcel of the capitalist mode of production and consumption. In this media environment, sociology has to be entertaining, exotic, maintain common sense and contribute to increased viewer ratings. Tester thus insists that "if sociology is to appear before publics through the media it will be necessarily shaped by values that are external to it and specific to a heterogeneous environment". Consequently, sociology wanting to become public finds itself in a paradoxical Catch-22 situation – it cannot become truly public without the media but it cannot become truly public through the media either. Tester therefore draws a somewhat dramatic, provocative and surprising conclusion from this ambivalence towards the media as vehicles for public sociology: "Sociology is most likely to play a part in the constitution of 'us' (a public) if the struggle to appear in the media is given up and if there is a refusal to collaborate with the media environment". Instead of collaborating with the media, Tester asks of sociology that it is and remains committed to the vocation of a 'principled sociology'.

Finally, the book contains a list of recommended readings for those interested in pursuing discussing or practicing public sociology or in excavating ideas on public sociology from the grand and rich historical treasury chest of sociology. Thus, the book aspires to inspire – it asks the reader to consider how – and also why – his or her own sociological practice may become relevant to the public, it nudges him or her to make their own research results available to public scrutiny and last but not least making such results applicable to wider public issues. So when it comes to public sociology, it is a matter of practicing rather than preaching and I will therefore like to repeat the poignant words from my favourite musical *The Rocky Horror Show*: "Don't dream it – be it!". I also wish to end this introduction to public sociology with Max Weber's insightful finale to his famous essay "Science as a Vocation" in which he opposed the tarrying and yearning procrastinations of those who are satisfied to postpone until tomorrow what should be done today:

> Nothing is gained by yearning and tarrying alone, and we shall act differently. We shall set to work and meet the 'demands of the day' in human relations as well as in our vocation. This, however, is plain and simple, if each finds and obeys the demon who holds the fibers of his very life (Weber 1919/1948:156).

And so, this book on public sociology seeks to engage each and every practicing sociologist in finding and obeying each their own demon – and preferably a public demon.

References

Bauman, Zygmunt (1987): *Legislators and Interpreters – On Modernity, Post-Modernity and Intellectuals*. Cambridge: Polity Press.

Bauman, Zygmunt (1992): *Intimations of Postmodernity*. London: Routledge.

Bauman, Zygmunt (1998): "Sociological Enlightenment – For Whom, About What?". *Dansk Sociologi*, 9 (special issue):43-54.

Bauman, Zygmunt (2002a): *Society Under Siege*. Cambridge: Polity Press.

Bauman, Zygmunt (2002b): "Pierre Bourdieu – or the Dialectics of Vita Contemplative and Vita Activa". *Revue Internationale de Philosophie*, 220:179-193.

Becker, Howard S. (1967): "Whose Side are We On?". *Social Problems*, 14 (3):239-247.

Bellah, Robert N., Richard Madsen, William M. Sullivan, Ann Swidler & Steven M. Tipton (1985/1996): "Appendix: Social Science as Public Philosophy", in *Habits of the Heart: Individualism and Commitment in American Life*. Berkeley, CA: University of California Press.

Bottomore, Tom (ed.)(1975): *Crisis and Contention in Sociology*. London: Sage Publications.

Boudon, Raymond (1980): *The Crisis in Sociology: Problems of Sociological Epistemology*. New York: Columbia University Press.

Burawoy, Michael (2004): "Public Sociology: Contradictions, Dilemmas and Possibilities". *Social Forces*, 82 (4):1603-1618.

Burawoy, Michael (2005a): "2004 ASA Presidential Address – For Public Sociology". *American Sociological Review*, 70 (1):4-28.

Burawoy, Michael (2005b): "For Public Sociology". *British Journal of Sociology*, 56 (2):259-294.

Burawoy, Michael (2005c): "The Return of the Repressed: Recovering the Public Face of U.S. Sociology, One Hundred Years On". *Annals of the American Academy of Political and Social Science*, 600 (1):68-85.

Cole, Stephen (ed.)(2001): *What's Wrong with Sociology?* New Brunswick, NJ: Transaction Books.

Davies, Philip (2004): "Sociology and Policy Science: Just in Time?". *British Journal of Sociology*, 55 (3):447-450.

Deflem, Mathieu (2004): "Letter to the Editor ('The Proper Role of Sociology in the World at Large')". *The Chronicle Review*, October 1. Available at http://www.cas.sc.edu/socy/faculty/deflem/zchronRev.html.

Friedrichs, Robert W. (1970): *A Sociology of Sociology*. New York: Free Press.

Gans, Herbert J. (1988): "Sociology in America: The Discipline and the Public". *American Sociological Review*, 54 (1):1-16.

Gans, Herbert J. (2002): "More of Us Should Become Public Sociologists". *ASA Footnotes* available at http://www.asanet.org/footnotes/julyaugust02/fn10.html.

Gibbons, Michael et al. (1994): *The New Production of Knowledge*. London: Sage Publications.

Giddens, Anthony (1976): *New Rules of Sociological Method*. London: Hutchinson.

Giddens, Anthony (1990): *The Consequences of Modernity*. Cambridge: Polity Press.

Gouldner, Alvin W. (1962): "Anti-Minotaur: The Myth of a Value-Free Sociology". *Social Problems*, 9 (3):199-213.

Habermas, Jürgen (1991): *The Structural Transformation of the Public Sphere*. Cambridge, MA: MIT Press.

Holmwood, John (2007): "Sociology as Public Discourse and Professional Practice: A Critique of Michael Burawoy". *Sociological Theory*, 25 (1):46-66.

Horowitz, Irving L. (1994): *The Decomposition of Sociology*. New York: Oxford University Press.

Jacobsen, Michael Hviid (2006a): "Kommentar: Fra himmelske højder – om klassikerkulten, intellektuelle ikoner og teoritendensen". *Dansk Sociologi*, 17 (3-4):105-116.

Jacobsen, Michael Hviid (2006b): "Sociologiens 'død'? Dødens sociologi – manifest for stimuleringen af den sociologiske fantasi i fragmentationens tidsalder". *Sosiologi i dag*, 36 (4):62-96.

Jacobsen, Michael Hviid (2007): "En diagnose over dansk sociologi – hvorfor sociologiens umulighed er sociologiens mulighed". *Dansk Sociologi*, 18 (3):109-121.

Kalleberg, Ragnvald (2005): "What Is 'Public Sociology'? Why and How Should It Be Made Stronger?". *British Journal of Sociology*, 56 (3):387-393.

Korpi, Walter (1990): "Om undran inför sociologerna". *Sociologisk Forskning*, 27 (3):2-10.

Kuhn, Thomas S. (1970): *The Structure of Scientific Revolutions*. Chicago: University of Chicago Press.

Lee, Alfred McClung (1976): "Sociology for Whom?". *American Sociological Review*, 41:925-936.

Lynd, Robert S. (1939): *Knowledge for What? The Place of Social Science in American Culture*. Princeton, NJ: Princeton University Press.

Machlup, Fritz (1956): "The Inferiority Complex in the Social Sciences", in Mary Sennholz (ed.): *On Freedom and Free Enterprise: Essays in Honor of Ludwig von Mises*. Princeton, NJ: Van Nordstrand.

MacRae, Donald G. (1964): "The Crisis of Sociology", in Jack H. Plumb (ed.): *Crisis in the Humanities*. Harmondsworth: Penguin Books.

Mills, Charles Wright (1949): *The New Men of Power*. New York: Harcourt Brace.

Mills, Charles Wright (1959): *The Sociological Imagination*. New York: Oxford University Press.

Mills, Charles Wright (1960): *Images of Man: The Classical Tradition in Sociological Thinking*. New York: George Braziller Inc.

Mokrzycki, Edmund (1983): *Philosophy of Science and Sociology: From the Methodological Doctrine to Research Practice*. London: Routledge & Kegan Paul.

Nowotny, Helga et al. (2001): *Rethinking Science: Knowledge and the Public in an Age of Uncertainty*. Cambridge: Polity Press.

Phillips, Derek L. (1971): *Knowledge from What? Theories and Methods in Social Research*. Chicago: Rand McNally & Company.

Posner, Richard A. (2001): *Public Intellectuals*. Harvard, MA: Harvard University Press.

Poupeau, Franck & Thierry Discepolo (2004): "Scholarship with Commitment: On the Political Engagements of Pierre Bourdieu". *Constellations*, 11 (1):76-96.

Rappert, Brian (1999): "The Uses of Relevance: Thoughts on a Reflexive Sociology". *Sociology*, 33 (4):705-723.

Reynolds, Larry T. & Janice M. Reynolds (eds.)(1970): *The Sociology of Sociology*. New York: David McKay Company.

Rojek, Chris & Bryan S. Turner (2000): "Decorative Sociology: Towards a Critique of the Cultural Turn". *Sociological Review*, 48 (4):629-648.

Rule, James B. (1978): "Models of Relevance: The Social Effects of Sociology". *American Journal of Sociology*, 84 (1):78-98.

Schram, Sanford F. & Brian Caterino (eds.)(2006): *Making Political Science Matter: Debating Knowledge, Research and Method*. New York: New York University Press.

Sennett, Richard (1977): *The Fall of Public Man*. New York: W. W. Norton & Company.

Shapiro, Ian (2005): *The Flight from Reality in the Human Sciences*. Princeton, NJ: Princeton University Press.

Sorokin, Pitirim (1956): *Fads and Foibles in Modern Sociology*. Chicago: Henry Regnery Company.

Stinchcombe, Arthur L. (1994): "Disintegrated Disciplines and the Future of Sociology". *Sociological Forum*, 9 (2):279-291.

Stokes, Donald E. (1997): *Pasteur's Quadrant: Basic Science and Technological Innovation*. New York: Brookings Institution Press.

Tittle, Charles R. (2004): "The Arrogance of Public Sociology". *Social Forces*, 82 (4):1639-1643.

Tonboe, Jens (2003): "Vedkommende sociologi", in Michael Hviid Jacobsen (ed.): *Sociologiske visioner – sytten bidrag fra en sociologisk brydningstid*. Århus: Systime Academic.

Turner, Stephen P. & Jonathan H. Turner (1990): *The Impossible Science: An Institutional Analysis of American Sociology*. Newbury Park, CA: Sage Publications.

Warner, Michael (2002): *Publics and Counterpublics*. New York: Zone Books.

Weber, Max (1919/1948): "Science as a Vocation", in Hans H. Gerth & Charles Wright Mills (eds.): *From Max Weber: Essays in Sociology*. London: Routledge.

Wolfe, Alan (1989): *Whose Keeper? Social Science and Moral Obligation*. Berkeley, CA: University of California Press.

Wolfe, Alan (1992): "Weak Sociology/Strong Sociologists: Consequences and Contradictions of a Field in Turmoil". *Social Research*, 59 (4):759-779.

Znaniecki, Florian (1940): *The Social Role of the Man of Knowledge*. New York: Harper.

Notes

1. Although the term 'public sociology' was in fact coined by Herbert J. Gans in a 1988 presidential address to the American Sociological Association (see Gans 1989).

2. It is interesting to observe how 'public sociology', as a sociological debate on how to make sociology more public, has to a large degree remained an American preoccupation. Although several outsiders have started to comment and write on matters of public sociology, the American touch is still unmistakable. In Scandinavia, for example, the debate on public sociology has remained meagre – in fact almost entirely absent – compared to the attention public sociology has received in the US.

3. It has been my position – and continues to be my position – in these debates that the often-heard claims of a current disciplinary crisis or fragmentation of sociology should rather be regarded simply as *pluralisation* and that the postulated disciplinary dissolution and decomposition is better viewed as *multiplication* (see Jacobsen 2006b, 2007). Therefore, the proposed 'impossibility' of sociology as a science (Turner & Turner 1990) is, as I see it, unfounded. In fact, the impossibility of sociology is exactly its possibility; its very grounds for survival and its bulwark against scientific stagnation.

4. In his lifetime C. Wright Mills, for example, conjured up six different major publics in society based on the diversified American public/political arena in the 1940s. He mentioned the following: the far left, the independent left, the liberal centre, the communists, the practical right and the sophisticated conservatives (Mills 1949). Undoubtedly, today's late modern society contains, at least, as many different publics, if not many more. Moreover, Mills's publics were all political or ideological publics whereas the existence of non-political publics is indeed also an option, perhaps especially in our thoroughly depoliticized times.

5. I wish to thank Jonas Larsen of Aalborg University for inspirational discussions of this topic and for assisting me in coining these concepts.

6. Let me clarify in order to avoid misunderstanding: I am in no way whatsoever opposed to individual sociologists or groups of sociologists specializing in or focusing on selected parts of the public, perhaps even infinitesimal or marginalized minorities, but I believe that sociology – as a distinctive discipline, as a 'science of society' – must aspire seek to reach, to research and to be relevant to the wider public of the so-called 'normal population'. Alternatively, sociology is in danger of turning into a miniaturistic or exoticized enterprise.

The Fall of Public Sociology

~

Ottar Brox

The title of this essay implies that there once was a public sociology, but that we do not have it any longer. But if you expect nostalgic laments with the message that everything, including sociology, was better half a century ago, you will be disappointed. The tools of the trade are without any doubt far better now than what they were in the 1950s, the students receive better education and many more grants are available for training researchers. But that has not, however, given us a better *public* sociology.

What do our fellow citizens have a right to expect from sociologists and our colleagues in the other social sciences? My simple point of departure is that the general public has a legitimate interest in our work, just like professional colleagues and the authorities or organizations which finance our projects. In the same sense as we do our best to be positively reviewed or quoted by senior colleagues, and deliver the reports that we have been paid for in due time, we have a duty to our fellow citizens to make our work relevant to the maintenance of public goods or to the solution of public problems.

Most of you have probably heard the widespread popular opinion of sociology as the art of expressing 'common sense', i.e. stating what everybody knows, in terms that nobody understands.

Today, it may be a valid generalization as far as much conventional sociology is concerned, but many of us have experiences that give us hopes that the discipline can be "a solvent of doxa" – to borrow Loïc Wacquant's apt expression.[1] 'Common sense' is very often widespread *taken for granted* opinions – e.g. shared by political opponents – that do not survive critical and empirical examination.

An important reason why I, relatively late in life, chose social science, was a little article by the Norwegian criminologist Nils Christie, attacking the generally shared opinion that alcoholised, homeless people represented a street cleansing problem, which was attempted solved by the police picking them up and sending them to a work camp for 18 months. Christie found out that their own opinion of this was that they where sentenced for being poor as people with enough money could get drunk without being sent to what in reality was a prison in the countryside. The true function of our profession is not the legitimation of 'common sense', but rather the opposite: to examine commonly held opinions to find out if they contain truth and what they do to the society that we have in common, i.e. to 'dissolve doxa'.

Michael Burawoy, to whom Michael Hviid Jacobsen refers in his introduction, defines public sociology as sociology *in dialog with the general public*.[2] It exists beside *professional*, *policy* and *critical* sociologies, of which the first is responsible for what I referred to as 'the tools of the trade', i.e. development of social theory and methodology. Policy sociology is what gives most of us bread and butter. Burawoy defines it as working for a contract partner, such as an arm of government that wants to have a policy evaluated, or a businessman who wants to know the preferences of his customers. Where I part with Burawoy, who seem to accept a peaceful coexistence between public and policy sociology, is just at this junction: I hope to show that *policy sociology will have to be truly public*. Otherwise there is a great risk that it simply may become a dangerous tool in the hands of the power-holders. If we are able to *socialise* policy sociology, i.e. make it public, it may even serve as a *critical* discipline, an adjective which Burawoy reserves for a sociology which reflects upon the *ends* or *goals* of social life, rather than merely looking at the *means*. This is the main message that I will try to convey in what follows.

But first some introductory remarks: There are two aspects of 'public' that should be in focus when we discuss the public interest in the social sciences. One is the public *discourse*: do sociologists help to improve our common ability to discuss social problems and arrive at practical solutions? The other aspect is derived from the classical dichotomy *public/private*: does the discipline help us to maintain public goods, i.e. common resources, redistribution arrangements or access to knowledge, art, recreation and other goods that should be accessible to all members of society?

In the present ideological climate, our common or *collective* interests tend to be neglected in the competition with the interests of individuals, business corporations and other actors, i.e. exactly those whose interests are taken care of in policy sociology.

Individual rights are far better protected in the law books than the rights that we as citizens may have in common. Private property rights are protected in the constitutions of most countries, whereas common rights to resources can be taken away and privatized by administrative decision-making. This is in fact what the Norwegian authorities have done to the fishing population of the northern coast, assisted by social scientists engaged in policy research.

As Mancur Olson demonstrated in *The Logic of Collective Action*, even if we all may benefit from collective goods, we profit most by being free riders, and leave the *costs* of collective action to others. We hire lawyers and other professionals to take care of our *intensive* private interests, but leave it to amateurs in socially responsible citizen groups to fight for the *diffuse* interests that we all have in common. But from our recent history we may learn that it has not always been like that: The Nordic welfare democracies were developed by *public* men and women, more concerned with the quality of our common society than with their personal bank accounts. Or to avoid moralizing: Working for the public good was simply more rewarding than building a fortune in stocks and options. And their contemporaries were far more concerned with their actions in the public sphere than with their fortunes, public images or the qualities of their personal selves.

One of those who did his best to teach me sociology in the early 1960s was the Norwegian sociologist Vilhelm Aubert. He was a *public man* in the sense that to him it seemed to be self-evident that the use of our discipline was to find the causes of poverty, crime, ethnic discrimination, excessive inequality and suffering, and use the knowledge generated to enlighten the public in the hope that our society could be improved to function better for *all* its members. When I was preparing this lecture, I went through his most important books in the hope of finding quotes to illustrate my point. But there were few if any heroic statements to the effect that he wanted to speak for the grassroots or act as a castigator of those in power. It is rather that his program for a truly public sociology permeates all his texts and his selection of problems to study. His personal participation in many aspects of society inspired him to ask those questions the answers to which he chose to spend his life and his professional resources to find. In this sense, he was an old-fashioned intellectual in the Enlightenment tradition. Even if he tried to locate funds that could be used to finance the project of a young colleague, he did not 'adapt to the market' for social research. And nota bene: Regardless of how a project was financed, nobody should tell him beforehand what *aspect* of a problem that deserved to be in focus. That was something that he expected to find out through his empirical work, whether he studied court cases or isolated Saami villages. And what he found out in his research endeavours, he wanted to tell as many as possible of his fellow citizens, in the hope that knowledge mattered. Almost a half century has passed since my generation of social scientists met Vilhelm Aubert as a teacher. Much has happened to our professions since then.

To clarify what I refer to in the somewhat dramatic title of this presentation, i.e. the 'fall' or degeneration of the social sciences, as seen from the viewpoint of the general public, I have to be as concrete as possible and use illustrative examples. In the Nordic countries, and certainly elsewhere as well, the disciplines in question have been thoroughly reorganised during the past decennia. Institutes of applied social sciences have been established for many thematic fields, such as substance abuse, child protection, regional development, consumer affairs and many others, and of course, many more people are today engaged in social research. To apply Michael Burawoy's aforementioned categories, we can safely say that the tremendous growth has been in *policy* sociology and in other social sciences that offer their services to public and private organizations. The available funds are much larger than in Vilhelm Aubert's days, but so is the competition for grants and research contracts. And not only independent institutes compete for these funds, as universities and colleges are encouraged by the educational authorities to find money in the market – at any rate in my own country.

This would indeed be very well if competition generated an ever-increasing quality of the output – as it should, according to fashionable and hegemonic theories. I am not today concerned with the number of internationally published articles or citations, as my theme is the *public* interest in our products. Compared to the 1960s, we have to admit that it is very low, and of course especially if we take the greatly increased volume into consideration. A very small percentage of our numerous reports and publications trigger debates in the media. My own experience indicates that social sciences are quoted in the media mainly when bits and pieces of texts can be used opportunistically as arguments for a pre-conceived conclusion.

I am afraid that even if there is a lot of competition among the many different suppliers of policy sociology, it is not professional quality that differentiates between winners and losers in this market. There are certain indications that the road to success lies in developing arguments in favour with the contract partner who ordered and paid for the project.

Today, there are research institutes which *adapt* to the market for arguments to the extent that what I thought were the most elementary scientific rules are disregarded. If a public authority, an organization or a private business pays a scientific institution to carry through a project, they have of course a right to define the *problem* that should be examined. But they should not get involved in *how* the project should be executed. If the Department of Agriculture wants to find out what will be the likely long term structural effects of changing some hygiene rules for farmers, it should leave the choice of effects to be examined to the researcher. Or else it could be tempted to order us to focus only on the positive effects and disregard the negative. Loïc Wacquant formulates 'The First Commandment' to be obeyed by anybody involved in policy research: *Thou shalt not ask your own questions!* Today, there are indeed competitors in the applied social research market who accepts this kind of manipulation: When the national government, planning to liberalize the hydro energy market, traditionally controlled by the municipal or regional governments, which initiated and invested in the waterfalls, hired researchers to evaluate the policy, it could decide *which* consequences of liberalization should be examined, and – by implication – which ones that should be left in the dark.

Half a century ago, I was taught that *all* results of social research should be published, i.e. made available to the general public, of course within limits set by the rights of individuals to be protected. Now, the trend is towards a situation where the social scientist's contract partner can decide, which results of a project can be published, which implies that powerful actors can pay for the production and publication of *pro* arguments for e.g. an administrative innovation, or new rules of the economic game, and avoid public awareness of arguments *contra*.

Obviously, in a competitive market there is a risk that such practices will have a tendency to be adopted by others as soon as they are introduced. In Norway, leaders of market-dependent institutes of applied research have hinted that they may have to accept more control by those who finance projects. And, of course, more subtle mechanisms than direct orders, specified in a written contract, may be at work: Research organizations will learn how to produce reports which increase their chances to obtain new projects.

It should not be too difficult to see that sociological knowledge cannot be produced in accordance with the public interest if we allow this development to run its course. There are other reasons – beyond the necessity to protect our professional independence – why social scientists must fight against this type of control of our work. The development of a project should first of all be inspired and steered by our sociological imagination and our reflections as social beings, acting with the authority of adult citizens.

But the reason why we cannot accept anyone with political or economic power and vested interests to tell us how to operationalize projects or which aspects of a problem are of interest, can be derived from elementary social theory. Few social scientists today base their theorizing on the premises that society has been consciously constructed to serve certain interests, and even less than it can be planned according to any kind of blueprint. And I hope that only unprofessional ideologues go around believing that our society is the way it is because we – the citizens – want it like that.

To those of us who are as sceptical to Marxist utopianism as we are to Liberalist voluntarism, society can most fruitfully be considered as a complex aggregate of unintended and largely unanticipated consequences of many actors' more or less successful attempts at realising their projects. Even if actors are very different with regard to power and knowledge, no one is able to 'design', plan or even *predict* the development of this complex whole. Society does not suffer problems like poverty, deaths on the road or pollution because people want to hurt their fellow citizens, but because actors pursue whatever they are after without bothering to reflect too much on the less immediate and visible consequences of their actions. That is the other aspect of Adam Smith's important point: The baker's struggle to make money gives his neighbours the opportunity to buy bread, but may also pollute the air that they have to breathe. But it is not his intention to destroy the environment for his customers, just like he does not carry on with his baking for altruistic reasons. Citizen A delivers his merchandise by lorry to customers at the other end of town, and citizen B drives his car to visit his sick mother. They do what is necessary or good, but cooperate with others to make the city dirty and dangerous.

Within this framework, the possible utility of policy sociology, or more generally applied social research, must be to explore the whole range of possible or likely consequences of social actions like new legislation, development projects, and reorganization of business corporations or amalgamation of municipal units.

Policies, projects or new rules of the economic game will usually be motivated, explained or legitimated with reference to a *goal* of high priority. Examples may be that the goal of higher energy prices is reduction of carbon dioxide, like the goal of making fish quotas tradable is to improve the economy of fishermen, as taxes may be reduced to increase investments or minimum wages increased to reduce poverty.

Obviously, *one* consequence of higher fuel prices may be less carbon dioxide in the atmosphere. But most human acts have more than one consequence. And there is every reason to consider what is called 'goal' as simply the most attractive of a long list of possible consequences of human action. Generally, unintended implications may be more important than the so-called 'goals' in terms of consequences, e.g. contribute more problematic additions to the complex aggregate that we call society than the attractive aspects, which were used as arguments to get the proposal accepted.

Around 1990 the Norwegian government introduced a new regulation regime for the cod fisheries. The 'goal' or 'intention' was to avoid over-fishing and over-investment in this important industry, and the social scientists hired to evaluate the reform proposal were only asked to examine its potential to do just that. But very soon it turned out that the most important *consequence* was that most of the coastal population lost their traditional rights to the common resource which hundreds of fishing communities had as their only economic base.

I may not yet have achieved to spell out my conclusion in clear text: To make 'policy sociology' useful to society as a whole, and not only serve as a tool in the hands of the power-holders or special interests, our ambition must be to define, examine and make visible *all* kinds of unanticipated, wanted and unwanted consequences of proposed policies, material installations or other social actions with a potential to change the complex aggregate of externalities in which we live. I am not saying that it is easy or even possible to predict long term consequences of reforms like the new fishery regulation systems. But it should not be difficult to see that skilful attempts in this direction would be of more public interest than 'policy sociology' steered in detail by the well organized interest groups with the most intensive economic interests in the policy under scrutiny.

My most attentive readers will have noticed that I repeatedly have referred to 'social sciences' rather than simply sticking to 'sociology', as I may have promised in the title of this essay. The reason should be obvious by now: If our ambition is to spell out the most important consequences of a proposed reform, or evaluate it some time after its introduction, a sociologist will have to work together with colleagues from other disciplines. Otherwise there is a great risk that we will only see what we are trained to see. Policy research is by necessity interdisciplinary – or rather 'poly-disciplinary' – in the same sense as complex technological challenges are. A group of Nobel class physicists would never be able to place a man on the moon, but a *team* of good professionals from all the relevant disciplines did. And the task of producing the knowledge that we need in order to avoid that policies with the most perfect 'goals' generate poverty, crime, climatic disasters or ethnic conflicts is a challenge of comparative magnitude. A practical implication is, of course, that institutes doing policy research have to consist of people from all relevant disciplines, who are trained to work in poly-disciplinary teams.

Large applied research programmes are – at any rate in Norway – organized in a way that implies a great risk that they will be useless. A not quite hypothetical example could be a well-financed rural development programme, most likely generated through political unrest in the provinces about depopulation. A steering committee will be appointed, where all possible interest groups will be represented, such as agriculture, manufacturing industry, fisheries and the Department of Municipal Affairs. It should be noted that actors with *influence* and thus responsibility for the problem being studied will dominate the steering process and have opportunities to take care of their interests.

This committee will – in the present research market situation – have to select ten winners among one-hundred project proposals. The administrative personnel will, of course, have the applications evaluated by senior disciplinary colleagues of the applicants, but still, the political interests of the committee members may prevail against the strictly professional evaluations by persons who are not supposed to pass judgement on the practical relevance of the projects. Everybody with experience from this kind of decision-making processes will know that the immediate necessity will be to reduce the large bunch of applications. This implies that all the vested interest representatives in the committee can avoid production of knowledge that does not serve them or that may potentially annoy or hurt them. Hence, a project that might show that government support would have more effects on rural employment if it was shifted from agriculture to activities not so well represented in the steering committee can be weeded out early in the process. A majority of the committee will tend to welcome all opportunities to throw as many applications as possible into the waste basket, simply to get through with the job. The organization of applied social research must be a main reason why it has been so difficult to trace positive effects of the many costly programs carried through during the last decennium. It is also very likely that the quality of applications deteriorates when less than ten percent of these ever have a chance to be rewarded.

But it is not only strong vested interest groups and excessive bureaucracy that threatens to lead the social sciences in the wrong directions. There are indeed other reasons why the public, or many citizens' collective interests, are neglected in applied social science. I have in mind *internal* developments within the academic environments, processes that may be as important in making our work irrelevant to the general public as the external, political and economic incentives are.

I will now have to use examples from a very controversial and complex matter that is difficult to grapple with in all Nordic countries – i.e. immigration. Elsewhere, I have tried to show that the public discourse on immigration has made the practical problems involved more difficult to solve – quite contrary to experiences from other sectors, where a lively public discussion may bring forward more useful information and practicable solutions.[3] This can be explained with reference to the polarized or *schismogenetic* character of all debates on immigration. Participants on the pro-front do not really speak to their adversaries on the contra-front, and *vice versa*. The discussion does not aim at finding practical compromises, but is rather used as an opportunity for presentation of self, i.e. showing one's attractive moral qualities or one's concern for 'our own sick, poor and helpless old people'. The interventions on both sides must be understood as attempts at being more *pro* or *contra* immigration than others on one's own side. To the social scientist, the production of real knowledge becomes very difficult, as it is hardly possible to say anything about immigration publicly without being classified as belonging to one of these fronts.

From the point of view of the concerned citizens, who want relevant facts on which to base their opinion, social science does not seem to have very much to offer. It is indeed striking how often academic discussions on immigration matters stagnate because the participants cannot agree on factual matters – in spite of the large number of man-labour years spent on immigration research, which by the way also is steered by committees of the same kind as I have described above.

One example may be the effect of marriage pattern on the integration process: Do the inclinations of young Norwegians with parents from Pakistan to marry relatives born and reared in Pakistan imply delayed integration of this ethnic category? A priori, it seems to be a plausible hypothesis and it is indeed also supported by some researchers.[4] But other colleagues show strong reluctance to accept this as relatively reliable knowledge and it is not difficult to understand why: They simply fear that this is a piece of knowledge that may be used by the anti-immigrant front, for example to meddle in the private lives of individual immigrants and their children. The dismal implication for uninhibited production of knowledge should not be too difficult to see: Be careful when you select problems for research, or you risk finding things that can be misused by people whose agenda you do not like. If you carry out your duty to the general public, and try to communicate your knowledge in all kinds of media and fora, you run the risk of being placed in the anti-immigration front *by your colleagues*, which may in fact mean ostracism, i.e. being excluded from a community which you believed that you were a bona fide member for life. I am afraid that apart from some individual exceptions, Nordic social science has not taken advantage of the great opportunities that the age of immigration offers for understanding our own societies better, at the same time as we – as a whole – may have confused the general public rather than contributed to enlightenment.

At the beginning of this presentation, I tried to specify two important demands to a truly public sociology. Besides contributing to and enhancing the quality of the public discourse, it should also be concerned with the development and maintenance of collective goods, exposed as they are to be eroded in this age of individualism. And immigration as a theme is well suited to demonstrate this point.

It is indeed striking how most sociologists, anthropologists and other professionals from the social sciences focus on the *individual* immigrant, or the individual employer in need of foreign labour at the expense of the effects of immigration with regard to the collective interests of the national society of which many immigrants wish to become a member.

A simple example may be labour import, which should not be confused with granting asylum to people who have to flee from other countries or the reunification of families. Many social scientists as well as other commentators argue for the right of people from poor countries to work in the rich ones, as well as for the right of an employer to recruit foreigners at wages not acceptable to his fellow citizens. In this case, coalitions are formed which are able to create and maintain doxic conceptions of reality. In any labour-importing country there will be employer representatives lobbying for the right to hire foreign workers, and economic planners arguing for the necessity to import what they consider to be the minimum factor – the 'bottleneck' of the national economy – be it raw materials or labour. These participants in the discussion will usually be considered as belonging to the 'right' (conservative/liberalist) end of the political spectre, and in the case of economic planners, as non-political or strictly professional. But what makes the generally shared opinion on labour migration into *doxa* is that the political *left* usually represent no opposition, as socialists seem to be as much in favour of labour import as their political adversaries, basing their standpoint on humanistic arguments or on claims to international solidarity, defending the right of the individual migrants to improve their current standard of living. Trade unions generally accept labour import, even if they insist – usually in vain

– on equal pay for the migrants. The doxic agreement on the necessity or goodness of hiring foreigners is probably a brake on the trade unions' struggle to maintain the power of their members in the labour market.

Even the fast-growing right populist parties exploiting xenophobia seem to be in favour of labour migration – at any right in Norway – only on the condition that migrants are denied the social protection that all workers within the borders are supposed to have in the national labour legislation.

The positive attitude to labour migration seems to be global. The World Bank has recently published economic studies of the money flow from rich to poor countries, showing that remittances from labour migrants amount to much more than all kinds of development assistance lumped together. The figures are impressive. They may be read against the backdrop of increasing scepticism towards conventional aid programmes, implying that offering migrants jobs in the rich world may be more efficient international development aid than sending checks or experts to the poor countries. But they may also be read as a support of the increasing concern about *shortage of labour* in the developed parts of the world. Commentators tend to stress the willingness of migrants to perform work that natives of developed countries no longer want to do. Hence, the World Bank's calculations may be used to show that international labour migration is a good thing not only for employers, but also – on a massive scale – for the labour exporting countries. As the bank's main findings seem to support the whole range of economic interests and political opinions on international labour migration, one should not expect any intense collegial scrutiny of the professional work on which the conclusions are based. The doxic conception of reality is continually being reinforced.

Hence there is near to zero opposition to the import of labour in most of the Western European countries. The few dissenting voices sometimes heard are easily ignored, or, if crudely formulated, classified as xenophobic or otherwise immoral. They will usually be met with arguments that 'we' are rich enough to allow 'them' the opportunity to harvest a little of our enormous surplus.

As far as I know, very few social scientists have attempted to explore the possible unintended consequences of labour import for the maintenance of common goods or intangible collective arrangements in the importing countries. In the case of Norway, and probably in the other Nordic countries as well, it is easy to specify some of these collective goods: strong trade unions, small wage differences, traditional absence of 'working poor', near to full employment (in comparative terms) and decent public unemployment insurance. Collective goods of this kind cannot be taken for granted. They may easily evaporate if they are not consciously maintained and reformed.

As soon as one starts to explore the possible effects of labour imports on these aspects of the importing countries – "no holds barred", to quote C. Wright Mills – doxa begins to dissolve. We might start with one of the most important premises: *The rich countries must import workers to perform the jobs that the natives no longer want*. In most Western European cities, those who keep the environment clean, in-doors as well as out-doors, look and quite often speak different languages from the natives whose offices and hospitals they wash and whose garbage they collect. Does anybody really believe that garbage bags would accumulate on the sidewalks and fill up the streets if there were no immigrants there to remove them? Is it not rather likely that the city council would have to raise wages or improve work conditions enough to make natives apply for the jobs?

A few years ago, the Norwegian labour authorities found out that there were too few nurses' helpers on the market and consequently proposed to import tens of thousands from poorer countries like the Philippines. It should be easy to see that there were alternative solutions: Young natives who may have considered nursing as an occupation found out that it was less attractive than the available alternatives – such as working in boutiques or coffee shops.

By improving wages and working conditions in nursing homes, more young people might have chosen this occupation. Import of workers who are willing to accept conditions that natives refuse implies *maintaining* the low level of attractivity. Thus, this solution maintains the need to find applicants abroad and widen the gap between nurses' helpers and other occupational groups. Importing workers does not seem to *solve* a shortage of labour in an industry or occupation, but rather *enlarge* the problem that it is supposed to solve. When business or public organizations are unable to attract enough applicants to vacant jobs, the obvious interpretation is that people consider them unattractive as compared to available alternatives. Hiring workers from poor countries will then tend to maintain the low level of attractiveness, while jobs in branches that *adapt* to a tighter domestic labour market continue to improve as options. This dynamic process towards certain occupations becoming 'immigrant jobs' must have taken place in many developed countries.

In general terms, labour import *generates* 'jobs that the natives no longer want'. The implication is larger wage differences, which is a general cause behind many social problems, and of course higher profits in the private sector. Trade unions generally have problems organizing industries hiring labour migrants. There can be no doubt that changes in the distribution of income is the most important effect of labour import in the import country, both directly by changing the power balance in the labour market and – in the longer run – by weakening the institutions that must be credited for the relative equality in some Western European countries.

The redistributive institutions of the democratic welfare states have been developed through more than a century of political enlightenment, organizing and struggle – towards the goal formulated by T. H. Marshall as 'social citizen rights', i.e. that every citizen has the right to a reasonable share of what is produced within the national borders. But the increased concentration on individual and universal rights by modern social scientists implies that the maintenance of the welfare state as a collective good seems to be neglected. The Norwegian sociologist Per V. Hagesæther assumes that the nation state is an untenable construction and questions the collective rights of all citizens of some western countries to a share in the collective product of the national society. He refers to the fact that other privileges and inequalities have been abolished, like slavery and aristocracy: "But an inherited privilege persists: To be born in a rich, western country….". He is, however, an optimist, and refers to trends that give him the hope that "the privileges connected with being the citizen of a western national state may be less legitimate".[5] In clear text, this must mean that a citizen of, say, a Nordic country must be willing to compete for jobs with people with very bad alternatives, and thus with very little bargaining power.

To social scientists like Hagesæther, and there are many of them, attempts to maintain borders between national labour markets implies maintaining global injustices. But globalizing the labour market of a welfare state with a more or less social-democratic history is first of all an operation which changes the power relationship between employers and employees. The wishful dream of our colleague implies dismantling the collective work of several generations of trade unionists, democratically elected politicians, intellectuals and public servants, who have built institutions to secure a certain degree of equal distribution of the national product. The long term consequence can only be that people will learn that politics does not matter, with the all too predictable results in terms of decreasing political participation and election turn-out.

The public discourse on labour migration shows that we do not utilise the potential of the social sciences to dissolve doxa, as they rather seem to reinforce untenable presumptions. As we have seen, The World Bank has convinced everybody that the individual remittances from labour migrants are much more important to the poor of the world than all kinds of development assistance lumped together. But again, our focus on the individual makes us forget the *collective* interests of people in poor countries. We are – for good humanitarian reasons – very much concerned with the dismal situation of Moroccans trying to get to Spain to pick tomatoes at African wage levels. But it may exactly be the opportunities of the Spanish vegetable industry to hire labour at wages that no Spaniard would accept that destroy Morocco's own possibilities to develop a vegetable industry. In the very fast-growing volume of labour migration literature, you can look in vain for references to effects on the development prospects of the labour-exporting countries.

It is not unreasonable to consider The World Bank calculations and the increasing general consensus about labour migration as the most promising kind of development assistance as similar to what we used to call *ideology* a few years ago. To the hegemonic forces in the emerging global economic system, labour migration is an opportunity to use labour from the poor countries to change the distribution of power in the rich ones. It is understandable that The World Bank want it to appear as a transfer of values from the rich to the poor. But it is hard to see why the international community of sociologists – and our colleagues in the other social sciences – appear to be so unable to come up and contribute with alternative understandings of the modern world to the general public.

It is very important for me not to be misunderstood with regard to this point: I am not appealing to fellow social scientists to 'take sides', confront 'the establishment' or engage in the class struggle. I would applaud a colleague who e.g. argued in favour of illegal immigration, because it would give employers cheaper production factors, which is supposed to be good for the economy. His or her work would help bringing the theme into the public arena and stimulate the public discourse. What helps to make sociology irrelevant to our fellow citizens is that we tend to stay away from controversial themes, like the monkeys who would not see, hear or say anything evil. I know of social scientists who are reluctant to discuss problematic aspects of labour import, as they are afraid to provide arguments for political entrepreneurs exploiting xenophobic opinions. But we should rather let the prospects for controversies trigger our *professional curiosity*, as we are more likely to produce interesting and useful knowledge by getting involved in controversies than looking for more or less plausible, but usually also more or less ineffective arguments for good causes – like reducing grass root xenophobia.

Rather than sum up – in the sense of repeating what I have already said – I will try to connect my message to Michael Hviid Jacobsen's proposed expansion of the concept of 'double hermeneutic' in his introduction. Not only the younger Anthony Giddens has experienced the futility of telling political and administrative authorities what one has found out as a sociologist and what should be done about it. Sociologists speak on low volume, and those in power do not have to listen to us. Our professional work will only have any effect if it is picked up and interpreted on the grass root level by neighbourhood groups, environmental organizations, even political parties (in multiparty systems), or any congregation of people trying to do something about their life situation. Politicians do not have to listen to professors, but they do indeed have motives to listen to mobilised voters – the public.

But this kind of impact depends upon how we zoom in on the problems that we decide to work at. Rather than accept the formulation of 'social problems' delivered by the Department of Social Affairs, we will have to interpret the discourse going on around kitchen tables, in pubs and in letters to the editor. If we shall ever carry forth the hope of being used in people's struggles for a better life, we will have to understand their life situations as well as they themselves understand it, and in addition be able to make it understandable to others. A project may start by empirically based interpretation of the social actors that we study, and it is successfully carried through when these actors interpret our analysis and use it for their own purposes.

NOTES

1. See his "Critical Thought as a Solvent of Doxa" at http://transform.eipcp.net/transversal/0806/wacqant/en.
2. Michael Burawoy: "The World Needs Public Sociology". *Sosiologisk Tidsskrift*, 12 (3):255-272 (2004).
3. See my book: *"Jeg er ikke rasist, men…": Hvordan får vi våre meninger om innvandrere og innvandring?* Oslo: Gyldendal 1991. An English version appeared as "Schismogenetic Conflicts", in Tore Slaatta (ed): *Media and the Transition of Collective Identities*. Department of Media and Communication, University of Oslo, 1996.
4. See Unni Wikan: *Mot en ny norsk underklasse*, pp. 114-118. Oslo: Gyldendal, 1995, and Inger-Lise Lien: *Ordet som stempler djevlene*, pp. 149-152. Oslo: Aventura, 1997.
5. Pål V. Hagesæther: "Gift deg proforma i dag – og bli helt i morgen?". *Samtiden*, 2 (2005).

MAKING SOCIOLOGY MATTER
- Phronetic Sociology as Public Sociology

~

Bent Flyvbjerg

INTRODUCTION

If we want to empower and re-enchant sociological research, we need to do three things. First, we must drop all pretence, however indirect, at emulating the success of the natural sciences in producing cumulative and predictive theory, for their approach simply does not work in sociology or any of the other social sciences.[1] Second, we must address problems that matter to groups in the local, national and global communities in which we live, and we must do it in ways that matter; we must focus on issues of context, values and power, as advocated by great social scientists from Aristotle and Machiavelli to Max Weber and Pierre Bourdieu. Finally, we must effectively and dialogically communicate the results of our research to our fellow citizens, the 'public', and carefully listen to their feedback. If we do this – focus on specific values and interests in the context of particular power relations – we may successfully transform sociological research into an activity performed in public for publics, sometimes to clarify, sometimes to intervene, sometimes to generate new perspectives, and always to serve as eyes and ears in ongoing efforts to understand the present and to deliberate about the future. We may, in short, arrive at sociology research that matters.

What I describe below as 'phronetic sociological research' is an attempt to arrive at such sociology. I would like to emphasize at the outset, however, that this effort should be considered as one among many possible, as a first approximation that will undoubtedly require further theoretical and methodological refinement, just as it will need to be developed through further practical employment in actual sociological studies. Despite such qualifications, I hope the reader will agree that given what is at stake – sociology that matters – the attempt at reforming such research is indeed worthwhile.

What Is Phronetic Sociology?

Phronetic sociological research is an approach to the study of organizations based on a contemporary interpretation of the classical Greek concept *phronesis*. Following this approach, phronetic sociologists study society and social organization with an emphasis on values and power. In this presentation I will first clarify what *phronesis* and phronetic sociology is. Second, I will attempt to tease out the methodological implications of this research approach.[2]

Aristotle is the philosopher of *phronesis* par excellence. In Aristotle's words, *phronesis* is an intellectual virtue that is "reasoned, and capable of action with regard to things that are good or bad for man".[3] *Phronesis* concerns values and goes beyond analytical, scientific knowledge (*episteme*) and technical knowledge or know how (*techne*) and it involves judgments and decisions made in the manner of a virtuoso social actor. I will argue that *phronesis* is commonly involved in practices of society and, therefore, that any attempts to reduce sociological research to *episteme* or *techne* or to comprehend them in those terms are misguided.

Aristotle was explicit in his regard of *phronesis* as the most important of the three intellectual virtues: *episteme*, *techne*, and *phrone-*

sis. *Phronesis* is most important because it is that activity by which instrumental rationality is balanced by value-rationality, to use the terms of German sociologist Max Weber; and because, according to Aristotle and Weber, such balancing is crucial to the viability of any social unit, from the family to the state. A curious fact can be observed, however. Whereas *episteme* is found in the modern words 'epistemology' and 'epistemic', and *techne* in 'technology' and 'technical', it is indicative of the degree to which scientific and instrumental rationality dominate modern thinking and language that we no longer have a word for the one intellectual virtue, *phronesis*, which Aristotle and other founders of the Western tradition saw as a necessary condition of successful social organization and as the most important prerequisite to such organization.

ARISTOTLE ON *EPISTEME*, *TECHNE* AND *PHRONESIS*

The term 'epistemic science' derives from the intellectual virtue that Aristotle calls *episteme*, and which is generally translated as 'science' or 'scientific knowledge'.[4] Aristotle defines *episteme* in this manner:

> [S]cientific knowledge is a demonstrative state, (i.e., a state of mind capable of demonstrating what it knows) ... i.e., a person has scientific knowledge when his belief is conditioned in a certain way, and the first principles are known to him; because if they are not better known to him than the conclusion drawn from them, he will have knowledge only incidentally – this may serve as a description of scientific knowledge.[5]

Episteme concerns universals and the production of knowledge that is invariable in time and space and achieved with the aid of analytical rationality. *Episteme* corresponds to the modern scientific ideal as expressed in the natural sciences. In Socrates and Plato, and subsequently in the Enlightenment tradition, this scientific ideal became dominant. The ideal has come close to being the only legitimate view of what constitutes genuine science, such that even intellectual activities like sociology and other social sciences, which are not and probably never can be scientific in the epistemic sense, have found themselves compelled to strive for and legitimate themselves in terms of this Enlightenment ideal.[6]

Whereas *episteme* resembles our ideal modern scientific project, *techne* and *phronesis* denote two contrasting roles of intellectual work. *Techne* can be translated into English as 'art' in the sense of 'craft'; a craftsperson is also an *art*isan. For Aristotle, both *techne* and *phronesis* are connected with the concept of truth, as is *episteme*. Aristotle says the following regarding *techne*:

> [S]ince (e.g.) building is an art [*techne*] and is essentially a reasoned productive state, and since there is no art that is not a state of this kind, and no state of this kind that is not an art, it follows that art is the same as a productive state that is truly reasoned. Every art is concerned with bringing something into being, and the practice of an art is the study of how to bring into being something that is capable either of being or of not being ... For it is not with things that are or come to be *of necessity* that art is concerned [this is the domain of *episteme*] nor with natural objects (because these have their origin in themselves) ... Art ... operate[s] in the sphere of the variable.[7]

Techne is thus craft and art, and as an activity it is concrete, variable and context-dependent. The objective of *techne* is the application of technical knowledge and skills according to a pragmatic instrumental rationality, what Michel Foucault calls "a practical rationality governed by a conscious goal".[8] Sociology practiced as *techne* would, for example, be a type of consulting aimed at better running organizations or other parts of society by means of instrumental rationality, where 'better' is defined in terms of the values and goals of those who employ the consultants, sometimes in negotiation with the latter.

Whereas *episteme* concerns theoretical *know why* and *techne* denotes technical *know how*, *phronesis* emphasizes practical knowledge and practical ethics. *Phronesis* is often translated as 'prudence' or 'practical common sense'. Let us again examine what Aristotle has to say:

> We may grasp the nature of prudence [*phronesis*] if we consider what sort of people we call prudent. Well, it is thought to be the mark of a prudent man to be able to deliberate rightly about what is good and advantageous ... But nobody deliberates about things that are invariable ... So ... prudence cannot be a science or art; not science [*episteme*] because what can be done is a variable (it may be done in different ways, or not done at all), and not art [*techne*] because action and production are generically different. For production aims at an end other than itself; but this is impossible in the case of action, because the end is merely doing *well*. What remains, then, is that it is a true state, reasoned and capable of action with regard to things that are good or bad for man ... We consider that this quality belongs to those who understand the management of households or states (original emphasis).[9]

Please note that the word 'management' is not mine, but that of the original English translator of Aristotle's text. The person possessing practical wisdom (*phronimos*) has knowledge of how to manage in each particular circumstance that can never be equated with or reduced to knowledge of general truths about managing. *Phronesis* is a sense or a tacit skill for doing the ethically practical rather than a kind of science. For Plato, rational humans are moved by the cosmic order; for Aristotle they are moved by a sense of the proper order among the ends we pursue. This sense cannot be articulated in terms of theoretical axioms, but is grasped by *phronesis*.[10]

One might get the impression in Aristotle's original description of *phronesis* that *phronesis* and the choices it involves in concrete management are always good. This is not necessarily the case. Choices must be deemed good or bad in relation to certain values and interests in order for good and bad to have meaning. Phronetic sociology is concerned with deliberation about values and interests.

In sum, the three intellectual virtues – *episteme, techne,* and *phronesis* – can be characterized as follows:

Episteme   Scientific knowledge: Universal, invariable, context-independent. Based on general analytical rationality. The original concept is known today by the terms 'epistemology' and 'epistemic'. Sociology practiced as *episteme* is concerned with uncovering universal truths about society and social organization.

Techne   Craft/art: Pragmatic, variable, context-dependent. Oriented toward production. Based on practical instrumental rationality governed by a conscious goal. The original concept appears today in terms such as 'technique', 'technical' and 'technology'. Sociology practiced as *techne* is consulting aimed at running society or social organizations better by means of instrumental rationality, where 'better' is defined in terms of the values and goals of those who employ the consultants, sometimes in negotiation with the latter.

Phronesis   Ethics: Deliberation about values with reference to praxis. Pragmatic, variable, context-dependent. Oriented toward action. Based on practical value-rationality. The original concept has no analogous contemporary term. Sociology practiced as *phronesis* is concerned with deliberation about (including questioning of) values and interests.

The Priority of the Particular

Phronesis concerns the analysis of values – "things that are good or bad for man" – as a point of departure for managed action. *Phronesis* is that intellectual activity most relevant to praxis. It focuses on what is variable, on that which cannot be encapsulated by universal rules, on specific cases. *Phronesis* requires an interaction between the general and the concrete; it requires consideration, judgment, and choice.[11] More than anything else, *phronesis* requires *experience*. About the importance of specific experience Aristotle says:

> [P]rudence [*phronesis*] is not concerned with universals only; it must also take cognizance of particulars, because it is concerned with conduct, and conduct has its sphere in particular circumstances. That is why some people who do not possess theoretical knowledge are more effective in action (especially if they are experienced) than others who do possess it. For example, suppose that someone knows that light flesh foods are digestible and wholesome, but does not know what kinds are light; he will be less likely to produce health than one who knows that chicken is wholesome. But prudence is practical, and therefore it must have both kinds of knowledge, or especially the latter.[12]

Here, again, Aristotle is stressing that in practical management (in this case the management of health, which was a central concern for the ancient Greeks), knowledge of the rules ("light flesh foods are digestible and wholesome") is inferior to knowledge of the real cases ("chicken is wholesome"). Some of the best management schools, such as Harvard Business School, have understood the importance of cases over rules and emphasize case-based and practical teaching. Such management schools may be called Aristotelian; whereas schools stressing theory and rules may be called Platonic.

Some interpretations of Aristotle's intellectual virtues leave doubt as to whether *phronesis* and *techne* are distinct categories, or whether *phronesis* is just a higher form of *techne* or know-how.[13]

Aristotle is clear on this point, however. Even if both *phronesis* and *techne* involve skill and judgment, one type of intellectual virtue cannot be reduced to the other; *phronesis* is about value judgment, not about producing things.

Similarly, in other parts of the literature one finds attempts at conflating *phronesis* and *episteme* in the sense of making *phronesis* epistemic. But insofar as *phronesis* operates via a practical rationality based on judgment and experience, it can only be made scientific in an epistemic sense through the development of a theory of judgment and experience. In fact Alessandro Ferrara has called for the "elaboration of a theory of judgment" as one of "the unaccomplished tasks of critical theory".[14] In line with Jürgen Habermas, Ferrara says that a theory of judgment is necessary in order to avoid contextualism, although he also notes that such a theory "unfortunately is not yet in sight".[15] What Ferrara apparently does not consider is that a theory of judgment and experience is not in sight because judgment and experience cannot be brought into a theoretical formula. Aristotle warns us directly against the type of reductionism that conflates *phronesis* and *episteme*.

With his thoughts on the intellectual virtues, Aristotle emphasizes properties of intellectual work, which are central to the production of knowledge in the study of social organizations and other social phenomena. The particular and the situationally dependent are emphasized over the universal and over rules. The concrete and the practical are emphasized over the theoretical. It is what Martha Nussbaum calls the "priority of the particular" in Aristotle's thinking.[16] Aristotle practices what he preaches by providing a specific example of his argument, viz. light flesh foods vs. chicken. He understands the 'power of example'. The example concerns the management of human health and has as its point of departure something both concrete and fundamental concerning human functioning. Both aspects are typical of many Classical philosophers.

We will return to these points later. At this stage, we simply conclude that despite their importance, the concrete, the practical and the ethical have been neglected by modern science. Today, one would be open to ridicule if one sought to support an argument using an example like that of Aristotle's chicken. The sciences are supposed to concern themselves precisely with the explication of universals, and even if it is wrong, the conventional wisdom is that one cannot generalize from a particular case.[17] Moreover, the ultimate goal of scientific activity is supposedly the production of theory. Aristotle is here clearly anti-Socratic and anti-Platonic. And if modern theoretical science is built upon any body of thought, it is that of Socrates and Plato. We are dealing with a profound disagreement here.

Below, we will look at specific examples of phronetic social scientific/sociological research. More generally, in contemporary social science, Pierre Bourdieu's 'fieldwork in philosophy' and Robert Bellah's 'social science as public philosophy' are examples of such intellectual pursuits that involve elements of *phronesis*.[18] Bourdieu explicitly recognizes Aristotle as the originator of the habitus concept, which is so centrally placed in Bourdieu's work, and he sees the practical knowledge that habitus procures as being analogous to Aristotle's *phronesis*.[19] In philosophy, Richard Bernstein's and Stephen Toulmin's 'practical philosophy' and Richard Rorty's 'philosophical pragmatism' are also phronetic in their orientation, as are Michel Foucault's 'genealogies'.[20] As pointed out by Rorty, 'philosophy' in this interpretation is precisely what a culture becomes capable of when it ceases to define itself in terms of explicit rules, and becomes sufficiently leisured and civilized to rely on inarticulate know-how, to "substitute *phronesis* for codification".[21] Aristotle found that every well-functioning organization and society was dependent on the effective functioning of all three intellectual virtues – *episteme*, *techne*, and *phronesis*. At the same time, however, Aristotle emphasized the crucial importance of *phronesis*, "for the possession of the single virtue of prudence [*phronesis*] will carry with it the possession of them all".²² *Phronesis* is most important, from an Aristotelian point of view, because it is that intellectual virtue that may ensure the ethical employment of science (*episteme*) and technology (*techne*). Because *phronesis* today is marginalized in the intellectual scheme of things, scientific and technological development take place without the ethical checks and balances that Aristotle saw as all-important. This is a major problem in its own right.

Sociology and 'Real' Science

Regardless of the lack of a term for *phronesis* in our modern vocabulary, the principal objective for sociological research with a phronetic approach is to perform analyses and derive interpretations of the status of values and interests in societies or social organizations aimed at social change. The point of departure for classical phronetic research can be summarized in the following three value-rational questions:

1) Where are we going?
2) Is this development desirable?
3) What, if anything, should we do about it?

The 'we' here consists of those sociologists asking the questions and those who share the concerns of the researchers, including people in the social organization under study. Later, when I have discussed the implications of power for *phronesis*, I will add a fourth question:

4) Who gains and who loses, and by which mechanisms of power?

Sociologists who ask and provide answers to these questions use their studies not merely as a mirror for social organizations to reflect on their values, but also as the nose, eyes and ears of social organizations in order to sense where things may be going next and what, if anything, to do about it. The questions are asked with the realization that there is no general and unified 'we' in relation to which the questions can be given a final, objective answer. What is a 'gain' and a 'loss' often depend on the perspective taken, and one person's gain may be another's loss. Phronetic sociologists are highly aware of the importance of perspective and see no neutral ground, no 'view from nowhere', for their work.

It should be stressed that no one has enough wisdom and experience to give complete answers to the four questions, whatever those answers might be. Such a wisdom and experience should not be expected from sociologists, who are on average no more astute or ethical than anyone else. What should be expected, however, are attempts from phronetic sociologists to develop their partial answers to the questions. Such answers would be input to the ongoing dialogue about the problems, possibilities and risks that societies or social organizations face and how things may be done differently.

A first step in achieving this kind of perspective in sociology is for researchers to explicate the different roles of research as *episteme*, *techne* and *phronesis*. Today's researchers seldom clarify which of these three roles they are practicing. The entire enterprise is simply called 'research' or 'science', even though we are dealing with quite different activities. It is often the case that these activities are rationalized as *episteme*, even though they are actually *techne* or *phronesis*. As argued previously, it is not in their role of *episteme* that one can argue for the value of sociology and other social sciences. In the domain in which the natural sciences have been strongest – the production of theories that can explain and accurately predict – the social sciences, including sociology, have been weakest. Nevertheless, by emphasizing the three roles, and especially by reintroducing *phronesis*, we see there are other possibilities for sociology and other social sciences. The oft-seen image of impotent social sciences versus potent natural sciences derives from their being compared in terms of their epistemic qualities. Yet, such a comparison is misleading, for the two types of science have their respective strengths and weaknesses along fundamentally different dimensions. As mentioned previously, the social sciences, in their role as *phronesis*, are strongest where the natural sciences are weakest.[23]

It is also as *phronesis* that sociologists and other social sciences can provide a counterweight to tendencies toward relativism and nihilism. The importance of *phronesis* renders the attempts of sociology and social science to become 'real' theoretical science doubly unfortunate; such efforts draw attention and resources away from those areas where they could make an impact and into areas where they do not obtain, never have obtained and probably never will obtain any significance as genuinely normal and predictive sciences.

Methodological Guidelines for Phronetic Sociology

What, then, might a set of methodological guidelines for phronetic sociology look like? This question will be the focus of the remainder of this paper. I would like to stress immediately that the methodological guidelines summarized below should not be seen as imperatives; at most they are cautionary indicators of direction. Let me also mention that undoubtedly there are ways of practising phronetic sociology other than those outlined here. The most important issue is not the individual methodology involved, even if methodological questions may have some significance. It is more important to get the result right – to arrive at sociology that effectively deals with deliberation, judgment and praxis in relation to the four value-rational questions mentioned above, rather than being stranded with sociology that vainly attempts to emulate the natural sciences.

As mentioned earlier, few scholars seem to have reflected explicitly on the comparative strengths and weaknesses of research practised as either *episteme, techne* or *phronesis*. Even fewer are actually conducting research on the basis of such reflection, and fewer still have articulated the methodological considerations and guidelines for *phronesis*-based research. In fact, it seems that researchers doing *phronesis*-like work have a sound instinct for proceeding with their research and are not involving themselves in methodology. Nonetheless, given the interpretation of the actual and potential role of sociology, as outlined above, it is essential for the development of such research that methodological guidelines be elaborated.

The main point of departure for explicating methodological guidelines for phronetic sociology is a reading of Aristotle and Michel Foucault,[24] supplemented with readings of other thinkers – mainly Pierre Bourdieu, Clifford Geertz, Alasdair MacIntyre and Richard Rorty – who emphasize phronetic before epistemic knowledge in the study of societies and social organization, despite important differences in other domains.[25]

Focusing on Values

By definition, phronetic sociologists focus on values and, especially, evaluative judgments; for example, by taking their point of departure in the classic value-rational questions: "Where are we going?", "Is it desirable?" and "What should be done?". The objective is to balance instrumental rationality with value-rationality and increase the capacity of a variety of human actors to think and act in value-rational terms. Asking value-rational questions does not imply a belief in linearity and continuous progress. The phronetic sociologist knows enough about power to understand that social progress is often complex, ephemeral and hard-won, and that setbacks are an inevitable part of social life. I shall return to the issue of power below.

Focusing on values, phronetic sociologists are forced to face questions of foundationalism versus relativism – that is, the view that there are central values that can be rationally and universally grounded versus the view that one set of values is as good as another. Phronetic sociologists reject both of these 'isms' and replace them with contextualism or situational ethics. Distancing themselves from foundationalism does not leave phronetic sociologists normless, however. They take their point of departure in their attitude to the situation in the social organization and society being studied. They seek to ensure that such an attitude is not based on idiosyncratic morality or personal preferences, but on a common view among a specific reference group to which the social researchers refer. For phronetic sociologists, the socially and historically conditioned context – and not the universal grounding that is desired but not yet achieved by certain scholars, constitutes the most effective bulwark against relativism and nihilism.[26] Phronetic sociologists realize that our sociality and history is the only foundation we have, the only solid ground under our feet; and that this socio-historical foundation is fully adequate for our work as sociologists.

As regards validity, phronetic sociology is based on interpretation and is open for testing in relation to other interpretations and other research. But one interpretation is not as good as any other, which would be the case for relativism. Every interpretation must be built upon claims of validity, and the procedures ensuring validity are as demanding for phronetic sociology as for any other activity in the social sciences. Phronetic sociologists also oppose the view that any one among a number of interpretations lacks value because it is 'merely' an interpretation. As emphasized by Alexander Nehamas, the key point is the establishment of a *better* option, where 'better' is defined according to sets of validity claims.[27] If a new interpretation appears to better explain a given phenomenon, that new interpretation will replace the old one – until it, too, is replaced by a new and yet better interpretation. This is typically a continuing process, not one that terminates with 'the right answer'. Such is the procedure that a community of sociologists would follow in working together to put certain interpretations of social life ahead of others (see also the section on 'dialogue' below). The procedure does not describe an interpretive or relativistic approach. Rather, it sets forth the basic ground rules for any social inquiry, inasmuch as social science and philosophy have not yet identified criteria by which an ultimate interpretation and a final grounding of values and facts can be made.

Placing Power at the Core of Analysis

Aristotle, the philosopher of *phronesis* par excellence, never elaborated his conception of *phronesis* to include explicit considerations of power. Hans-Georg Gadamer's authoritative and contemporary conception of *phronesis* also overlooks issues of power.[28] Yet, as Richard Bernstein points out, if we are to think about what can be done to the problems, possibilities and risks of our time, we must advance from the original conception of *phronesis* to one explicitly including power.[29] Unfortunately, Bernstein himself has not integrated his work on *phronesis* with issues of power. Phronetic sociological inquiry, however, can only be complete if it deals with issues of power. I have therefore made an attempt to develop the classic concept of *phronesis* to a more contemporary one, which accounts for power.[30]

Besides focusing on the three value-rational questions mentioned above, which are the classical Aristotelian questions, a contemporary reading of *phronesis* also poses questions about power and outcomes: "Who gains and who loses?", "Through what kinds of power relations?", "What possibilities are available to change existing power relations?", "Is it desirable to do so?" and "What are the power relations among those who ask the questions?". Phronetic sociologists pose these questions with the intention of avoiding the voluntarism and idealism typical of so much ethical thinking. The main question is not only the Weberian: "Who governs?", as posed by Robert Dahl and most other students of power. It is also the Nietzschean question: "What 'governmental rationalities' are at work when those who govern govern?".[31] With these questions and with the focus on value-rationality, phronetic sociologists relate explicitly to a primary context of values and power. Combining the best of a Nietzschean-Foucauldian interpretation of power with the best of a Weberian-Dahlian one, the analysis of power is guided by a conception of power that can be characterized by six features:

1) Power is seen as productive and positive, and not only as restrictive and negative.
2) Power is viewed as a dense net of omnipresent relations, and not only as being localized in 'centres', organizations and institutions, or as an entity one can 'possess'.
3) The concept of power is seen as ultradynamic; power is not merely something one appropriates, it is also something one reappropriates and exercises in a constant back-and-forth movement within the relationships of strength, tactics and strategies inside of which one exists.
(4) Knowledge and power, truth and power, rationality and power are analytically inseparable from each other; power produces knowledge, and knowledge produces power.
(5) The central question is *how* power is exercised, and not merely *who* has power, and *why* they have it; the focus is on process in addition to structure.
(6) Power is studied with a point of departure in small questions, 'flat and empirical', not only, nor even primarily, with a point of departure in 'big questions'.[32]

Analyses of social power following this format cannot be equated with a general analytics of every possible power relation in society or social organizations. Other approaches and other interpretations are possible. They can, however, serve as a possible and productive point of departure for dealing with questions of power in doing *phronesis*.

Getting Close to Reality

Donald Campbell, Charles Lindblom and others have noted that the development of sociology and other types of social research is inhibited by the fact that researchers tend to work with problems in which the answer to the question "If you are wrong about this, who will notice?" is usually "Nobody".[33] Mary Timney Bailey calls the outcome of such research "'so what' results".[34] Phronetic sociologists seek to transcend this problem of relevance by anchoring their research in the context studied and thereby ensuring what Gadamer called a hermeneutic 'fusion of horizons'. This applies both to contemporary and historical sociological studies. For contemporary studies researchers get close to the social organization, phenomenon or group that they study during data collection and remain close during the phases of data analysis, feedback and publication of results. Combined with the above-mentioned focus on relations of values and power, this strategy typically creates interest in the research by parties outside the research community. These parties will test and evaluate the research in various ways. Phronetic sociologists will consciously expose themselves to positive and negative reactions from their surroundings and are likely to derive benefit from the learning effect, which is built into this strategy. In this way, the phronetic sociologist becomes a part of the phenomenon studied without necessarily 'going native' or the project becoming simple action research. Action researchers and anthropologists who have gone native typically identify with the people they are studying; they adopt the perspective and goals of those studied and use research results in an effort to achieve these goals. This is not necessarily the case for phronetic sociologists who at all times, in the service of truth, retain the classic academic freedom to problematize and be critical of what they see.

Phronetic sociologists performing historical studies conduct much of their work in those locales where the relevant historical materials are placed, and they typically probe deeply into archives, annals and individual documents. To the attentive researcher, archives will reveal knowledge whose visible body "is neither theoretical or scientific discourse nor literature, but a regular, daily practice".[35] In historical studies, as in contemporary ones, the objective is to get close to reality. *Wirkliche Historie* (real history), says Foucault, "shortens its vision to those things nearest to it".[36] C. Roland Christensen, arguably one of the fathers of the case method at Harvard University, expresses a similar attitude about his research by invoking Henry Miller to describe the approach taken by many case researchers:

> My whole work has come to resemble a terrain of which I have made a thorough, geodetic survey, not from a desk with pen and ruler, but by touch, by getting down on all fours, on my stomach, and crawling over the ground inch by inch, and this over an endless period of time in all conditions of weather.[37]

Emphasizing the Little Things

Phronetic sociologists begin their work by phenomenologically asking 'little questions' and focusing on what Clifford Geertz, with a term borrowed from Gilbert Ryle, calls 'thick description'.[38] This procedure may often seem tedious and trivial. Nietzsche and Foucault emphasize that it requires "patience and a knowledge of details", and it depends on a "vast accumulation of source material". Geertz explicates the dilemma involved in skipping minutiae. The problem with an approach that extracts the general from the particular and then sets the particular aside as detail, illustration, background or qualification, is, as Geertz says, that "it leaves us helpless in the face of the very difference we need to explore ... [it] does indeed simplify matters. It is less certain that it clarifies them".[39] Nietzsche, who advocates "patience and seriousness in the smallest things",[40] expresses a similar, though more radical, point regarding the importance of detail when he says that "[a]ll the problems of politics, of social organization, and of education have been falsified through and through ... because one learned to despise 'little' things, which means the basic concerns of life itself".[41]

The focus on minutiae, which directly opposes much conventional wisdom about the need to focus on 'important problems' and 'big questions', has its background in the fundamental phenomenological experience of small questions often leading to big answers. In this sense, phronetic organization research is decentred in its approach, taking its point of departure in organizational micropractices, searching for 'the Great' within 'the Small' and vice versa. "God is in the detail", the proverb says. "So is the Devil", the phronetic sociologist would add, doing work that is at the same time as detailed and as general as possible.

Looking at Practice Before Discourse

Through words and concepts we are continually tempted to think of things as being simpler than they are, says Nietzsche: "There is a philosophical mythology concealed in *language*" (original emphasis).[42] Michel Serres puts the matter even more succinctly, saying that "language has a disgust for things". Phronetic sociologists attempts to get beyond this problem. Thus, social practice or what people do in social life is seen as more fundamental than either discourse or theory – what people say. Johann Wolfgang von Goethe's phrase from *Faust, Am Anfang war die Tat* ("In the beginning was the deed"), could be the motto for phronetic sociology. It is echoed by Foucault who says that "discourse is not life"; regular, daily practice is life.[43] Phronetic sociology does not accept the maxim that there is nothing outside the text or outside discourse. Such an approach is too easy, giving its practitioners limitless sovereignty by allowing them to restate the text indefinitely.[44] Textual analysis must be disciplined by analysis of practices. Here, again, the position is not relativism but contextualism. The context of practices disciplines interpretation.

Phronetic sociology focuses on practical activity and practical knowledge in everyday situations in society. It *may* mean, but is certainly not limited to, a focus on known sociological, ethnographic and historical phenomena such as 'everyday life' and 'everyday people', with their focus on the so-called 'common'. What it *always* means, however, is a focus on the actual daily practices – common or highly specialized or rarefied – which constitute a given social field of interest, regardless of whether these practices constitute a stock exchange, a grassroots organization, a neighbourhood, a multinational corporation, an emergency ward or a local school board.

At the outset, social practices are recorded and described simply as events. "The question which I ask", says Foucault, "is not about codes but about events ... I try to answer this question without referring to the consciousness ... the will ... intention".[45] The phronetic sociologist records what happened "on such a day, in such a place, in such circumstances".[46] In *The Will to Power*, in describing his 'principles of a new evaluation', Nietzsche similarly says that when evaluating human action one should "take doing *something,* the 'aim,' the 'intention,' the 'purpose,' back into the deed after having artificially removed all this and thus emptied the deed" (emphasis in original).[47] Events and phenomena are presented together with their connections with other events and phenomena.[48] Discontinuities and changes in the meaning of concepts and discourses are documented. The hermeneutic horizon is isolated and its arbitrariness elaborated. At first, the sociologist takes no position regarding the truth-value and significance ascribed by participants to the social practices studied. No practice is seen as more valuable than another. The horizon of meaning is initially that of the single social practice. The researcher then attempts to understand the roles played by single practices studied in the total system of e.g. social and contextual relations. If it is established, for example, that a certain social practice is seen as rational according to its self-understanding – that is, by those practicing it, but not when viewed in the context of other horizons of meaning – the researcher then asks what role this 'dubious' rationality plays in a further context, historically, organizationally and politically, and what the consequences might be.

In addition to the Nietzschean removal of the doer from the deed, the focus on social practices as events also involves a self-removal on the part of the sociologists to allow them to disinterestedly inspect the *wirkliche Historie* of societies and social organizations. This distancing enables the researcher to master a subject matter even when it is hideous and when there is a 'brutality of fact' involved in the approach. This approach may, in turn, offend people who mistake the researcher's willingness to uncover and face the morally unacceptable for immorality. There may also be intensity and optimism, however, in facing even the pessimistic and depressing sides of power and human action in social organizations. The description of practices as events endures and gains its strength from detecting the forces that make life in the social organization work. And if the researcher uncovers a social reality that is ugly or even terrifying when judged by the moral standards, which, we like to believe, apply in many modern social organizations, this reality may also demonstrate something deeply human that may have to be faced squarely by people in the social organization, by sociologists and by the general public, if this reality is to be changed. Nietzsche acutely named this approach to research 'The Gay [*fröhliche*] Science', and he called those practising the approach 'free spirits', describing them as "curious to a vice, investigators to the point of cruelty, with uninhibited fingers for the unfathomable, with teeth and stomachs for the most indigestible ... collectors from morning till late, misers of our riches and our crammed drawers".[49] We need more 'free spirit' in sociology and this depiction of what they would be like may serve as a description of phronetic sociologists.

Studying Cases and Contexts

We have seen that Aristotle explicitly identifies knowledge of 'particular circumstances' as a main ingredient of *phronesis*.[50] Foucault similarly worked according to the dictum "never lose sight of reference to a concrete example".[51] Phronetic sociological research thus benefits from focusing on case studies, precedents and exemplars. *Phronesis* functions on the basis of practical rationality and judgment. As I have argued elsewhere, practical rationality and judgment evolve and operate primarily by virtue of in-depth case experiences.[52] Practical rationality, therefore, is best understood through cases – whether experienced or narrated – just as judgment is best cultivated and communicated via the exposition of cases. The significance of this point can hardly be overstated, which is why Richard Rorty, in responding to Max Weber's thesis regarding the modern 'disenchantment of the world', invokes John Dewey to say: "The way to re-enchant the world ... is to stick to the concrete".[53]

Context is important to case studies in society and social organizations. What has been called the 'primacy of context' follows from the observation that in the history of science, human action has shown itself to be irreducible to predefined elements and rules unconnected to interpretation.[54] Therefore, it has been impossible to derive praxis from first principles and theory. Praxis has always been contingent on context-dependent judgment, on situational ethics. It would require a major transformation of current philosophy and science if this view were to change, and such a transformation does not seem to be on the horizon. What Pierre Bourdieu calls the 'feel for the game' (a.k.a. *Fingerspitzengefühl*) is central to all human action of any complexity, including social action, and it enables an infinite number of 'moves' to be made, adapted to the infinite number of possible situations, which no rule-maker, however complex the rule, can foresee.[55] Therefore, the judgment, which is central to *phronesis* and praxis, is always context dependent. The minutiae, practices and concrete cases that lie at the heart of phronetic sociology must be seen in their proper contexts; both the small, local context, which gives phenomena their immediate meaning, and the larger, international and global context in which phenomena can be appreciated for their general and conceptual significance.[56] Given the role of context in phronetic sociology, insofar as such research is practised as applied ethics, it is situational ethics. The focus is on *Sittlichkeit* (ethics) rather than on *Moralität* (morality).

Asking 'How?' Doing Narrative

Phronetic sociological research focuses on the dynamic question 'How?' in addition to the more structural 'Why?'. It is concerned with both *Verstehen* (understanding) and *Erklären* (explanation). Outcomes of social phenomena are investigated and interpreted in relation to social processes. In the study of relationships of power in social organizations, we already emphasized with Foucault the how-question, "the little question … flat and empirical", as being particularly important. Foucault stressed that our understanding will suffer if we do not start our analyses with a 'How?'.

Asking 'How?' and conducting narrative analysis are closely interlinked activities. Earlier we saw that a central question for *phronesis* is: "What should we do?". To this Alasdair MacIntyre answers: "I can only answer the question 'What am I to do?' if I can answer the prior question 'Of what story or stories do I find myself a part?'".[57] Thus, Nietzsche and Foucault see history as being fundamental to social science and philosophy, and criticize social scientists and philosophers for their lack of 'historical sense'.[58] The same may be said about sociological research and researchers. History is central to phronetic sociology in both senses of the word – that is, *both* as narrative containing specific actors and events, in what Clifford Geertz calls a story with a scientific plot; *and* as the recording of a historical development.[59] Narratology, understood as the question of "how best to get an honest story honestly told", is more important than epistemology and ontology.[60]

Several observers have noted that narrative is an ancient method and perhaps our most fundamental form for making sense of experience.[61] To MacIntyre, the human being is a 'story-telling animal', and the notion of a history is as fundamental a notion as is the notion of an action.[62] In a similar vein, Cheryl Mattingly points out that narratives not only give meaningful form to our experiences. They also provide us with a forward glance, helping us to anticipate situations even before we encounter them, allowing us to envision alternative futures.[63] Narrative inquiries into social organizations do not – indeed, cannot – start from explicit theoretical assumptions. Instead, they begin with an interest in a particular social phenomenon that is best understood narratively. Narrative inquiries then develop descriptions and interpretations of the phenomenon from the perspective of participants, stakeholders, researchers and others. In historical social analysis, both event and conjuncture are crucial, just as practices are studied in the context of several centuries, akin to what Fernand Braudel calls *longue durée*. The century-long view is employed in order to allow for the influence on current social practices of traditions with long historical roots, an influence that is often substantially more significant than is assumed in mainstream sociological research.[64]

Moving Beyond Agency and Structure

In an attempt to transcend the dualisms of agency/structure, hermeneutics/structuralism and voluntarism/determinism, phronetic sociologists focus on both actors and structures and on the relationship between the two.⁶⁵ Social actors and their practices are analyzed in relation to the structures of the social organization in question. And structures are analyzed in terms of agency – not for the two to stand in a dualistic, external relationship , but so structures can be part of, can be internalized in actors, and so actors can be part of, can be internalized in, structures. Understanding from 'within' the social organization and from 'without' are both accorded emphasis, which is what Bourdieu, in adapting the Aristotelian and Thomist concept of 'habitus' – a highly relevant concept for phronetic sociological research – calls "the internalization of externality and the externalization of internality".⁶⁶ Elsewhere, Bourdieu explicitly states that the use of the notion of habitus can be understood as a way of escaping the choice between "a structuralism without a subject and the philosophy of the subject".⁶⁷

As anyone who has tried it can testify, it is a demanding task to account simultaneously for the structural influences that shape the development of a given social phenomenon while crafting a clear, penetrating narrative or microanalysis of that phenomenon.⁶⁸ As Diane Vaughan has said, theorizing about actors and structures remains bifurcated.⁶⁹ Researchers generally tend to generate either macro-level or micro-level explanations, ignoring the critical connections. Empirical work follows the same pattern. Instead of social research that attempts to link macro-level factors and actors' choices in a specific social phenomenon, scholars tend to dichotomize. Structural analyses and studies of actors each receive their share of attention, but in separate projects, by separate researchers. Those who join structure and actor in empirical work most often do so by theoretical inference: data at one level of analysis are coupled with theoretical speculation about the other. Although issues of actor and structure combine with particular emphasis in social organizations and institutions, classic social-science research methodology is less developed for studying social organizations and institutions than for studying individuals and aggregate patterns.⁷⁰ Sociology carries the burden of this fact. Therefore, many sociologists may not be convinced that there is an escape from the duality of structural and individual analysis. They may believe there is no middle ground, for the very recalcitrance of the problem seems to attest to its intractableness.

There is mounting evidence, however, that the actor/structure connection is not an insurmountable problem. In fact, it may not be a problem at all, says Vaughan, but simply an artefact of data availability and graduate training.[71] And we now have excellent examples from other areas of the social sciences showing us how to integrate and move beyond the simple dichotomy of actors and structures. Clifford Geertz's classic description of the Balinese cockfight progressively incorporates practices, institutions and symbols from the larger Balinese social and cultural world in order to help the reader understand the seemingly localized event of the cockfight.[72] Robert Putnam and his associates similarly combine individual and structural analysis – as well as contemporary history and the history of the *longue durée* – in their attempt to explain the performance of modern, democratic institutions in Italy.[73] James Ferguson demonstrates how local, intentional development plans in Lesotho interact with larger, unacknowledged structures to produce unintended effects that are instrumental to the organization of 'development' and development agencies.[74] Michael Herzfeld throws new light on bureaucratic organization by studying what appear to be peculiar administrative practices in relation to structural explanations of the nation state.[75] And Stella Tillyard works from the basis of personal histories and family dynamics to incorporate the larger socioeconomic and political scene of the entire Hanoverian Age.[76] Like these scholars, phronetic sociologists deliberately seek information that will answer questions about the intermeshing of actors and structures in actual settings, in ways that dissolve any rigid and preconceived conceptual distinction between the two.[77]

Dialoguing with a Polyphony of Voices

Phronetic sociology is dialogical in the sense that it incorporates, and, if successful, is itself incorporated into, a polyphony of voices, with no one voice, including that of the researcher, claiming final authority. The goal of phronetic sociology is to produce input to the ongoing dialogue and praxis in relation to social organizations and social life, rather than to generate ultimate, unequivocally verified knowledge about the nature of social organizations and social life. This goal accords with Aristotle's maxim that in questions of praxis, one ought to trust more in the public sphere than in science.[78] Dialogue, however, is not limited to the relationship between researchers and the people they study in the field. The relevant dialogue for a particular piece of research typically involves more than these two parties – in principle anyone interested in and affected by the subject under study. Such parties may be dialoguing independently of researchers until the latter make a successful attempt at entering into the dialogue with their research. In other instances, there may be no ongoing dialogue initially, the dialogue being sparked by the work of phronetic researchers. In *Habits of the Heart*, Robert Bellah and his co-authors expressed their hope that "the reader will test what we say against his or her own experience, will argue with us when what we say does not fit, and, best of all, will join the public discussion by offering interpretations superior to ours that can then receive further discussion".[79] This hope is as fine an expression of the phronetic dialogical attitude as we will find for a specific piece of research. *Habits of the Heart* was ultimately successful in achieving its aims of entering into and intensifying debate in USA about American values.[80]

Thus, phronetic sociology explicitly sees itself as not having a privileged position from which the final truth can be told and further discussion arrested. We cannot think of an "eye turned in no particular direction", as Nietzsche says. "There is *only* a perspective seeing, *only* a perspective 'knowing;' and the *more* affects we allow to speak about one thing, the *more* eyes, different eyes, we can use to observe one thing, the more complete will our 'concept' of this thing, our 'objectivity,' be" (original emphasis).[81] Hence, 'objectivity' in phronetic sociology is not "contemplation without interest" but employment of "a *variety* of perspectives and affective interpretations in the service of knowledge" (original emphasis).[82]

The significance of any given interpretation in a dialogue will depend on the extent to which the validity claims of the interpreter are accepted, and this acceptance typically occurs in competition with other validity claims and other interpretations. The discourses in which the results of phronetic sociology are used have, in this sense, no special status, but are subordinated to the same conditions as any other dialogical discourse. If and when the arguments of researchers carry special weight it would likely derive not from researchers having access to a special type of validity claim, but from researchers having spent more time on and being better trained at establishing validity than have other social actors. We are talking about a difference in degree, not in kind. To the phronetic researcher, this is the reality of sociology, although some sociologists act as if validity claims can and should be given final grounding. The burden of proof is on them. By substituting *phronesis* for *episteme*, phronetic sociologists avoid this burden, impossible as it seems to lift.

Some people may fear that the dialogue at the centre of phronetic sociology, rather than evolving into the desired polyphony of voices, will all too easily degenerate into a shouting match, a cacophony of voices, in which the loudest carries the day. In phronetic sociology, the means of prevention is no different from that of other research: only to the extent that the validity claims of phronetic sociologists are accepted will the results of their research be accepted in the dialogue. Phronetic sociologists thus recognize a human privilege and a basic condition: meaningful dialogue in context. 'Dialogue' comes from the Greek *dialogos*, where *dia* means 'between' and *logos* means 'reason'. In contrast to the analytical and instrumental rationality, which lie at the cores of both *episteme* and *techne*, the practical rationality of *phronesis* is based on a socially conditioned, intersubjective 'between-reason'.

Examples of Phronetic Social Research

To summarize, the result of phronetic sociology is a pragmatically governed interpretation of the studied social practices. The interpretation does not require the researcher to agree with the actors' everyday understanding; nor does it require the discovery of some deep, inner meaning of the practices. Phronetic sociology is in this way interpretive, but it is neither everyday nor deep hermeneutics. Phronetic sociology is also not about, nor does it try to develop, theory or universal method. Thus, phronetic sociology is an analytical project, but not a theoretical or methodological one.

The following examples provided below serve as brief representations of examples in an emerging body of social research that contains elements of Aristotelian-Foucauldian *phronesis* as interpreted above. The examples are primarily related to organizational research as this field has been of particular interest to me. However, the examples could also be extracted from many other regions of the social sciences, including sociology. It must also be stressed again, however, that phronetic sociology may be practised in ways other than those described here, as long as they effectively deal with deliberation, judgment and praxis in relation to values and power, and as long as they answer the four value-rational questions mentioned above. In the organization of the firm and of accounting, the work of Peter Miller must be mentioned.[83] In the organization of science and technology, there is the work of Bruno Latour and Paul Rabinow.[84] And in the organization of government, there is Mitchell Dean's work.[85] The important work of Stewart Clegg has already been mentioned.

Examples also exist from more specialized fields of research such as the organization of consumption,[86] insurance and risk,[87] space and architecture,[88] policing,[89] poverty and welfare,[90] sexual politics,[91] and psychology.[92] Specifically in Scandinavia, the work of Tomas Brytting, Ulla Johansson and Svante Leijon on ethics, responsibility and the organization of labour and municipalities may serve as examples of phronetic organization research.[93] My own attempts at developing phronetic social research have been aimed at the organization of democracy and its institutions, public and private.[94]

One task of sociological research practised on the basis of the methodological guidelines presented here, is to provide concrete examples and detailed narratives of the ways in which power and values work in social organizations and with what consequences, and to suggest how power and values could be changed to work with other consequences. Insofar as social situations become clear, they are clarified by detailed stories of who is doing what to whom. Such clarification is a principal concern for phronetic sociology and provides the main link to praxis.

Phronetic sociology explores current practices and historic circumstances to find avenues to praxis. The task of phronetic sociology is to clarify and deliberate about the problems, possibilities and risks that different social organizations face, and to outline how things could be done differently – all in full knowledge that we cannot find ultimate answers to these questions or even to a single version of what the questions are.

REFERENCES

Abbott, Andrew (1992): "What Do Cases Do? Some Notes on Activity in Sociological Analysis", in Charles Ragin & Howard S. Becker (eds.): *What Is a Case? Exploring the Foundations of Social Inquiry*. Cambridge: Cambridge University Press.

Andler, Daniel (1998): "The Normativity of Context". Unpublished paper, Université Paris X, Nanterre.

Arendt, Hannah (1958): *The Human Condition*. Chicago: University of Chicago Press.

Aristotle (1976): *The Nicomachean Ethics* (abbreviated as *N.E.*). Harmondsworth: Penguin Books.

Bailey, Mary Timney (1992): "Do Physicists Use Case Studies? Thoughts on Public Administration Research". *Public Administration Review*, 52:47-54.

Bal, Mieke (1997): *Narratology: Introduction to the Theory of Narrative*. Toronto: University of Toronto Press.

Bartky, Sandra Lee (1990): *Femininity and Domination: Studies in the Phenomenology of Oppression*. New York: Routledge.

Bellah, Robert (1993): "Professionalism and Citizenship: Are They Compatible?". Paper presented at Wake Forest University, Winston-Salem, North Carolina, May 21.

Bellah, Robert N., Richard Madsen, William M. Sullivan, Ann Swidler & Steven M. Tipton (1985): *Habits of the Heart: Individualism and Commitment in American Life*. New York: Harper & Row.

Bellah, Robert N., Richard Madsen, William M. Sullivan, Ann Swidler & Steven M. Tipton (1991): *The Good Society*. New York: Alfred A. Knopf.

Bernstein, Richard (1985): *Beyond Objectivism and Relativism: Science, Hermeneutics and Praxis*. Philadelphia: University of Pennsylvania Press.

Bernstein, Richard (1989): "Interpretation and Solidarity: An Interview by Dunja Melcic". *Praxis International*, 9:201-219.

Bourdieu, Pierre (1977): *Outline of a Theory of Practice*. Cambridge: Cambridge University Press.

Bourdieu, Pierre (1988): *Homo Academicus*. Stanford, CA: Stanford University Press.

Bourdieu, Pierre (1990): *In Other Words: Essays Towards a Reflexive Sociology*. Cambridge: Polity Press.

Bourdieu, Pierre & Loïc J. D. Wacquant (1992): *An Invitation to Reflexive Sociology*. Chicago: University of Chicago Press.

Brytting, Tomas (2001): *Att vara som gud? Moralisk kompetens i arbetslivet*. Malmö: Liber.

Brytting, Tomas, Hans de Geer & Gunilla Silfverberg (1997): *Moral i verksamhet: Ett etiskt perspektiv på företag och arbete*. Stockholm: Natur och Kultur.

Calhoun, Craig (1994): "E. P. Thompson and the Discipline of Historical Context". *Social Research*, 61:233-243.

Campbell, Donald T. (1986): "Science's Social System of Validity-Enhancing Collective Belief Change and the Problems of the Social Sciences", in Donald W. Fiske & Richard A. Sweder (eds.): *Metatheory in Social Science: Pluralisms and subjectivities*. Chicago: University of Chicago Press.

Carr, David (1986): *Time, Narrative and History*. Bloomington: Indiana University Press.

Christensen, C. Roland & Abby J. Hansen (1987): "Teaching with Cases at the Harvard Business School", in Ronald C. Christensen & Abby J. Hansen (eds.): *Teaching and the Case Method*. Boston, MA: Harvard Business School Press.

Clegg, Stewart (1989): *Frameworks of Power*. Newbury Park, CA: Sage Publications.

Clegg, Stewart (1997): "Foucault, Power and Organizations", in Alan McKinlay & Ken P. Starkey (eds.): *Foucault, Management and Organization Theory: From Panopticon to Technologies of Self*. London: Sage Publications.

Coleman, James (1985): "Social Theory, Social Research and a Theory of Action". *American Journal of Sociology*, 91:1309-1335.

Collins, Randall (1980): "On the Microfoundations of Macrosociology". *American Journal of Sociology*, 86:984-1014.

Crush, Jonathan (1994): "Scripting the Compound: Power and Space in the South African Mining Industry". *Environment and Planning D: Society and Space*, 12:301-324.

Czarniawska, Barbara (1997): *Narrating the Organization: Dramas of Institutional Identity*. Chicago: University of Chicago Press.

Czarniawska, Barbara (1998): *A Narrative Approach to Organization Studies*. Thousand Oaks, CA: Sage Publications.

Dean, Mitchell (1991): *The Constitution of Poverty: Toward a Genealogy of Liberal Governance*. London: Routledge.

Dean, Mitchell (1999): *Governmentality: Power and Rule in Modern Society*. Thousand Oaks, CA: Sage Publications.

Devereux, Daniel T. (1986): "Particular and Universal in Aristotle's Conception of Practical Knowledge". *Review of Metaphysics*, 39:483-504.

Donzelot, Jacques (1979): *The Policing of Families*. New York: Pantheon.

Dreyfus, Hubert I. & Stuart E. Dreyfus (1990): "What is Morality: A Phenomenological Account of the Development of Expertise", in David Rasmussen (ed.): *Universalism vs. Communitarianism*. Cambridge, MA: MIT Press.

Dreyfus, Hubert I. & Paul Rabinow (eds.)(1982): *Michel Foucault: Beyond Structuralism and Hermeneutics*. Brighton: Harvester Press.

Engel, Susan (1999): *Context is Everything: The Nature of Memory*. New York: W. H. Freeman.

Eribon, Didier (1991): *Michel Foucault*. Cambridge, MA: Harvard University Press.

Ewald, François (1986): *L'etat providence*. Paris: B. Grasset.

Ewald, François (1996): *Histoire de l'etat providence: Les origines de la solidarite*. Paris: B. Grasset.

Fehn, Ann, Ingeborg Hoesterey & Maria Tatar (eds.)(1992): *Neverending Stories: Toward a Critical Narratology*. Princeton: Princeton University Press.

Fenno Jr., Richard F.. (1986): "Observation, Context and Sequence in the Study of Politics". *American Political Science Review*, 80:3-15.

Ferguson, James (1990): *The Anti-Politics Machine: 'Development', Depoliticization and Bureaucratic Power in Lesotho*. Cambridge: Cambridge University Press.

Ferrara, Alessandro (1989): "Critical Theory and Its Discontents: On Wellmer's Critique of Habermas". *Praxis International*, 8:305-320.

Ferrara, Alessandro (1999): *Justice and Judgement: The Rise and the Prospect of the Judgement Model in Contemporary Political Philosophy*. Thousand Oaks, CA: Sage Publications.

Fine, Gary Alan (1988): "On the Macrofoundations of Microsociology: Constraint and the Exterior Reality of Structure". Paper presented at the annual meetings of the American Sociological Association, Atlanta.

Flyvbjerg, Bent (1989): "Socrates Didn't Like the Case Method, Why Should You?", in Hans E. Klein (ed.): *Case Method Research and Application: New Vistas*. Needham, MA: World Association for Case Method Research and Application.

Flyvbjerg, Bent (1991): "Sustaining Non-Rationalized Practices: Body-Mind, Power and Situational Ethics: An interview with Hubert and Stuart Dreyfus". *Praxis International*, 1:93-113.

Flyvbjerg, Bent (1998): *Rationality and Power: Democracy in Practice*. Chicago: University of Chicago Press.

Flyvbjerg, Bent (2001): *Making Social Science Matter: Why Social Inquiry Fails and How It Can Succeed Again*. Cambridge: Cambridge University Press.

Flyvbjerg, Bent (2004): "Five Misunderstandings about Case Study Research", in Clive Seale, David Silverman, Jaber F. Gubrium & Giampetro Gobo (eds.): *Qualitative Research Practice*. London: Sage Publications.

Flyvbjerg, Bent, Nils Bruzelius & Werner Rothengatter (2003): *Megaprojects and Risk: An Anatomy of Ambition*. Cambridge: Cambridge University Press.

Foucault, Michel (1969): *Titres et travaux*. Pamphlet printed in fulfilment of requirements for candidacy at the Collège de France. Paris: privately printed.

Foucault, Michel (1972): "Le discours de toul". *Le Nouvel Observateur*, 372:15.

Foucault, Michel (1979): "My Body, This Paper, This Fire". *Oxford Literary Review*, 4:9-28.

Foucault, Michel (1981): "Questions of Method: An Interview". *I&C*, 8:3-14.

Foucault, Michel (1982): "The Subject and Power", in Hubert I. Dreyfus & Paul Rabinow (eds.): *Michel Foucault: Beyond Structuralism and Hermeneutics*. Brighton: Harvester Press.

Foucault, Michel (1984a): "Nietzsche, Genealogy, History", in Paul Rabinow (ed.): *The Foucault Reader*. New York: Pantheon.

Foucault, Michel (1984b): "Space, Knowledge, and Power: Interview with Paul Rabinow", in Paul Rabinow (ed.): *The Foucault Reader*. New York: Pantheon.

Foucault, Michel (1991): "Politics and the Study of Discourse", in Graham Burchell, Colin Gordon & Peter Miller (eds.): *The Foucault Effect: Studies in Governmentality*. Chicago: University of Chicago Press.

Gadamer, Hans-Georg (1975): *Truth and Method*. London: Sheed & Ward.

Geertz, Clifford (1973): *The Interpretation of Cultures*. New York: Basic Books.

Geertz, Clifford (1977): "Deep Play: Notes on the Balinese Cockfight", in Clifford Geertz: *The Interpretation of Cultures: Selected Essays*. New York: Basic Books.

Geertz, Clifford (1983): *Local Knowledge: Further Essays in Interpretive Anthropology*. New York: Basic Books.

Geertz, Clifford (1988): *Works and Lives: The Anthropologist as Author*. Stanford, CA: Stanford University Press.

Geertz, Clifford (1995a): *After the Fact: Two Countries, Four Decades, One Anthropologist*. Cambridge, MA: Harvard University Press.

Geertz, Clifford (1995b): "Disciplines". *Raritan*, 14:65-102.

Geertz, Clifford (1995c): "History and Anthropology". *New Literary History*, 21:321-335.

Giddens, Anthony (1982): "Hermeneutics and Social Theory", in Anthony Giddens: *Profiles and Critiques in Social Theory*. Berkeley, CA: University of California Press.

Giddens, Anthony (1984): *The Constitution of Society: Outline of the Theory of Structuration*. Cambridge: Polity Press.

Habermas, Jürgen (1984): *The Theory of Communicative Action*, Vol. 1. Boston, MA: Beacon Press.

Harcourt, Bernard E. (2001): *Illusion of Order: The False Promise of Broken Windows Policing*. Cambridge, MA: Harvard University Press.

Hardy, Cynthia & Stewart Clegg (1996): "Some Dare Call It Power", in Stewart Clegg, Cynthia Hardy & Walter R. Nord (eds.): *Handbook of Organization Studies*. London: Sage Publications.

Harrison, Paul Raymond (1989): "Narrativity and Interpretation: On Hermeneutical and Structuralist Approaches to Culture". *Thesis Eleven*, 22:61-78.

Heller, Agnes (1990): *Can Modernity Survive?* Berkeley, CA: University of California Press.

Henderson, David K. (1994). "Epistemic Competence and Contextualist Epistemology: Why Contextualism Is Not Just the Poor Person's Coherentism". *The Journal of Philosophy*, 91:627-649.

Herzfeld, Michael (1992): *The Social Production of Indifference: Exploring the Symbolic Roots of Western Bureaucracy*. Chicago: University of Chicago Press.

Johansson, Ulla (1998): *Om ansvar: Ansvarföreställningar och deras betydelse för den organisatoriska verkligheten*. Lund: Lund University.

Latour, Bruno (1996): *Aramis, or the Love of Technology*. Cambridge, MA: Harvard University Press.

Latour, Bruno (1999): *Pandora's Hope: Essays on the Reality of Science Studies*. Cambridge, MA: Harvard University Press.

Leijon, Svante (ed.)(1993): *God kommunal organisation: Lyssning, tolkning och handling*. KFi-rapport 22. Göteborg.

Leijon, Svante (1996): *Arbete i brytningstid: Tankar om tillvarons dualiteter*. BAS, Göteborg.

Lerner, Gerda (1997): *Why History Matters*. Oxford: Oxford University Press.

Lévi-Strauss, Claude & Didier Eribon (1991): *Conversations with Claude Lévi-Strauss*. Chicago: University of Chicago Press.

Lindblom, Charles E. (1990): *Inquiry and Change: The Troubled Attempt to Understand and Shape Society*. New Haven: Yale University Press.

Lindblom, Charles E. & David K. Cohen (1979): *Usable Knowledge: Social Science and Social Problem Solving*. New Haven, CT: Yale University Press.

Lord, Carnes & David K. O'Connor (eds.)(1991): *Essays on the Foundations of Aristotelian Political Science*. Berkeley, CA: University of California Press.

MacIntyre, Alasdair (1977): "Epistemological Crises, Dramatic Narrative and the Philosophy of Science". *Monist*, 60:453-472.

MacIntyre, Alasdair (1984): *After Virtue: A Study in Moral Theory*. Notre Dame: University of Notre Dame Press.

MacIntyre, Alasdair (1988): *Whose Justice? Which Rationality?* Notre Dame: University of Notre Dame Press.

MacIntyre, Alasdair (1990): *Three Rival Versions of Moral Enquiry: Encyclopaedia, Genealogy and Tradition*. London: Duckworth.

Mattingly, Cheryl (1991): "Narrative Reflections on Practical Actions: Two Learning Experiments in Reflective Storytelling", in Donald A. Schön (ed.): *The Reflective Turn: Case Studies In and On Educational Practice*. New York: Teachers College Press.

Miller, Henry (1941): "Reflections on Writing", in Henry Miller: *The Wisdom of the Heart*. New York: New Directions.

Miller, James (1993): *The Passion of Michel Foucault*. New York: Simon & Schuster.

Miller, Peter (1994): "Accounting and Objectivity: The Invention of Calculating Selves and Calculable Spaces", in Arthur Megil (ed.): *Rethinking Objectivity*. Durham: Duke University Press.

Miller, Peter & Nikolas Rose (1997): "Mobilising the Consumer: Assembling the Subject of Consumption". *Theory, Culture & Society*, 14:1-36.

Minson, Jeffrey (1993): *Questions of Conduct: Sexual Harassment, Citizenship and Government*. London: Macmillan.

Monk, Ray (1990): *Ludwig Wittgenstein: The Duty of Genius*. New York: Free Press.

Nehamas, Alexander (1985): *Nietzsche: Life as Literature*. Cambridge, MA: Harvard University Press.

Nietzsche, Friedrich (1966): *Beyond Good and Evil*. New York: Vintage Books.

Nietzsche, Friedrich (1968a): *The Anti-Christ*. Harmondsworth: Penguin Books.

Nietzsche, Friedrich (1968b): *The Will to Power*. New York: Vintage Books.

Nietzsche, Friedrich (1968c): *Twilight of the Idols*. Harmondsworth: Penguin Books.

Nietzsche, Friedrich (1969a): *Ecce Homo*. New York: Vintage Books.

Nietzsche, Friedrich (1969b): *On the Genealogy of Morals*. New York: Vintage Books.

Novak, Michael (1975): "'Story' and Experience", in James B. Wiggins (ed.): *Religion as Story*. Lanham, MD: University Press of America.

Nussbaum, Martha C. (1990): "The Discernment of Perception: An Aristotelian Conception of Private and Public Rationality", in Martha C. Nussbaum: *Love's Knowledge: Essays on Philosophy and Literature*. Oxford: Oxford University Press.

Procacci, Giovanna (1993): *Gouverner la misère: La question sociale en France (1789-1848)*. Paris: Éditions du Seuil.

Putnam, Robert D., Robert Leonardi & Raffaella Y. Nanetti (1993): *Making Democracy Work: Civic Traditions in Modern Italy*. Princeton, NJ: Princeton University Press.

Rabinow, Paul (1989): *French Modern: Norms and Forms of the Social Environment*. Cambridge, MA: MIT Press.

Rabinow, Paul (1996): *Making PCR: A Story of Biotechnology*. Chicago: University of Chicago Press.

Rabinow, Paul (1999): *French DNA: Trouble in Purgatory*. Chicago: University of Chicago Press.

Rabinow, Paul & William M. Sullivan (1987): "The Interpretive Turn: A Second Look", in Paul Rabinow & William M. Sullivan (eds.): *Interpretive Social Science: A Second Look*. Berkeley, CA: University of California Press.

Rasmussen, David (1995): "Rethinking Subjectivity: Narrative Identity and the Self". *Philosophy & Social Criticism*, 21:159-172.

Ricoeur, Paul (1984): *Time and Narrative*. Chicago: University of Chicago Press.

Rorty, Richard (1985): "Habermas and Lyotard on Postmodernity", in Richard J. Bernstein (eds.): *Habermas and Modernity*. Cambridge, MA: MIT Press.

Rorty, Richard (1991): *Philosophical Papers*. Cambridge: Cambridge University Press.

Rorty, Richard (1995): "Response to James Gouinlock", in Herman J. Saatkamp Jr., (ed.): *Rorty and Pragmatism: The Philosopher Responds to His Critics*. Nashville: Vanderbilt University Press.

Rose, Nikolas (1985): *The Psychological Complex: Psychology, Politics and Society in England, 1869-1939*. London: Routledge & Kegan Paul.

Rose, Nikolas (1996): *Inventing Our Selves: Psychology, Power and Personhood*. Cambridge: Cambridge University Press.

Rosen, Lawrence (1989): *The Anthropology of Justice: Law as Culture in Islamic Society*. Cambridge: Cambridge University Press.

Ruderman, Richard S. (1997): "Aristotle and the Recovery of Political Judgment". *American Political Science Review*, 91:409-420.

Schmidt, James (1985): *Maurice Merleau-Ponty: Between Phenomenology and Structuralism*. New York: St. Martin's Press.

Schram, Sanford F. & Brian Caterino (eds.)(2006): *Making Political Science Matter: Debating Knowledge, Research, and Method*. New York: New York University Press.

Seung, T. K. (1982): *Structuralism and Hermeneutics*. New York: Columbia University Press.

Sewell, William H., Jr. (1992): "A Theory of Structure: Duality, Agency, and Transformation". *American Journal of Sociology*, 98:1-29.

Shannon, Benny (1990): "What Is Context?". *Journal for the Theory of Social Behaviour*, 20:157-166.

Taylor, C. C. W. (1995): "Politics", in Jonathan Barnes (ed.): *The Cambridge Companion to Aristotle*. Cambridge: Cambridge University Press.

Taylor, Charles (1989): *Sources of the Self: The Making of the Modern Identity*. Cambridge, MA: Harvard University Press.

Tillyard, Stella (1994): *Aristocrats*. New York: Farrar, Straus & Giroux.

Toulmin, Stephen (1988): "The Recovery of Practical Philosophy". *The American Scholar*, 57:337-352.

van Maanen, John (1988): *Tales of the Field: On Writing Ethnography*. Chicago: University of Chicago Press.

Vaughan, Diane (1992): "Theory Elaboration: The Heuristics of Case Analysis", in Charles Ragin & Howard S. Becker (eds.): *What Is a Case?* Cambridge: Cambridge University Press.

NOTES

1. For the full argument, see Flyvbjerg (2001).
2. For an example of the practical implementation of phronetic sociology, I refer the reader to Flyvbjerg (1998). See also shorter examples in the main text of this paper.
3. Aristotle, *The Nicomachean Ethics* (hereafter abbreviated as *N.E.*):1140a24-b12, 1144b33-1145a11.
4. In the short space of this paper, it is not possible to provide a full account of Aristotle's considerations about the intellectual virtues of *episteme, techne,* and *phronesis*. Instead, I have focused upon the bare essentials, based on a reading of the original texts. A complete account would further elaborate the relations between *episteme, techne,* and *phronesis,* and the relationship of all three to *empeiria*. It would also expand on the relationship of phronetic judgments to rules, on what it means to succeed or to fail in the exercise of *phronesis,* and on the conditions that must be fulfilled if *phronesis* is to be acquired. For further discussion of these questions and of the implications of Aristotle's thinking for contemporary social science, see my discussion with Dreyfus & Dreyfus in Flyvbjerg (1991:101ff). See also MacIntyre (1984), Bernstein (1985), Heller (1990), Lord & O'Connor (1991) and Taylor (1995).
5. *N.E.*:1139b18-36.
6. For the full argument that social science can probably never be scientific in the epistemic sense, see Flyvbjerg (2001), Chapters 3 and 4.
7. *N.E.*:1140a1-23.
8. See Foucault (1984b:255).
9. *N.E.*:1140a24-b12.
10. See Taylor (1989:125, 148).
11. On the relationship between judgment and *phronesis,* see Ruderman (1997).
12. *N.E.*:1141b8-27.
13. For such an interpretation, with an unclear distinction between *phronesis* and *techne,* see Dreyfus & Dreyfus (1990). See also my discussion of this issue with the Dreyfus brothers in Flyvbjerg (1991:102-107).
14. See Ferrara (1989:319).
15. See Ferrara (1989:316). See also Ferrara (1999).
16. See Nussbaum (1990:66). See also Devereux (1986).
17. Regarding ways of generalizing from a single case, see Flyvbjerg (2004).
18. See Bourdieu (1990:28) and Bellah, Madsen, Sullivan, Swidler & Tipton (1985)(especially the Methodological Appendix, pp. 297ff).
19. See Bourdieu & Wacquant (1992:128).
20. See Bernstein (1985:40), Toulmin (1988:337) and Rorty (1991, 1995:94-95).
21. See Rorty (1991:25).
22. *N.E.*:1144b33-1145a11. For Aristotle, man [sic] has a double identity. For the 'human person', that is, man in politics and ethics, *phronesis* is the most important intellectual virtue. Insofar as man can transcend the purely human, contemplation assumes the highest place. *N.E.*:1145a6ff and 1177a12ff.
23. For discussion of this point and its theoretical and methodological implications, see Schram

& Caterino (2006).
24 For an interpretation of Foucault as a practitioner of *phronesis*, see Flyvbjerg (2001), Chapter 8, "Empowering Aristotle".
25 It should be mentioned that MacIntyre's Aristotle is substantially more Platonic than the Aristotle depicted by the others, and more Platonic than the interpretation given here. MacIntyre explicitly understands Aristotle "as engaged in trying to complete Plato's work, and to correct it precisely insofar as that was necessary in order to complete it". See MacIntyre (1988:94, 1990).
26 Nihilism is a theory promoting the state of believing in nothing or of having no allegiances and no purposes.
27 See Nehamas (1985:63).
28 See Gadamer (1975).
29 See Bernstein (1989:217).
30 See Flyvbjerg (2001) Chapters 7 and 8.
31 See also Clegg (1989, 1997) and Hardy and Clegg (1996).
32 See Foucault (1982:217).
33 See Campbell (1986:128-129), Lindblom & Cohen (1979:84) and Lindblom (1990). The quote in the text is from Campbell.
34 See Bailey (1992:50).
35 See Foucault (1969:4-5); here quoted from Eribon (1991:215).
36 See Foucault (1984a:89).
37 See Miller (1941:27); quoted in slightly different form in Christensen & Hansen (1987:18).
38 See Geertz (1973:6, 1983).
39 See Geertz (1995a:40). See also Geertz (1990, 1995b).
40 See Nietzsche (1968a:182, §59).
41 See Nietzsche (1969a:256, §10).
42 See Nietzsche (1968a:191, Appendix C).
43 After Wittgenstein had abandoned any possibility of constructing a philosophical theory, he suggested that Goethe's phrase from *Faust*, quoted in the main text, might serve as a motto for the whole of his later philosophy. See Monk (1990:305-306). The Foucault quote is from Foucault (1991:72). On the primacy of practices in Foucault's work, see also Foucault (1981:5) and Foucault quoted in Eribon (1991:214-216).
44 See Foucault (1979:27).
45 See Foucault (1991:59, 1981:6-7).
46 See Foucault (1972:15); here quoted from Miller (1993:191).
47 See Nietzsche (1968b:356, §675).
48 For more on eventualization, see Abbott (1992).
49 See Nietzsche (1966:55).
50 N.E.:1141b8-1141b27.
51 See Foucault (1969:7), quoted in Eribon (1991:216).
52 See Flyvbjerg (1989). See also MacIntyre (1977).
53 See Rorty (1985:173).
54 See Rabinow & Sullivan (1987:8). See also Henderson (1994).
55 See Bourdieu (1990:9).
56 For more on context, see Andler (1998), Calhoun (1994), Engel (1999), Fenno Jr. (1986) and

Shannon (1990: 157–166).
57 See MacIntyre (1984:216).
58 See Nietzsche (1968c:35, §1).
59 See Geertz (1988:114). See also Geertz (1995c), "History and Anthropology", with responses by Rosaldo and Lerner.
60 See Geertz (1988:9). In organization research, see van Maanen (1988) and Czarniawska (1997, 1998).
61 See Novak (1975:175) and Mattingly (1991:237). See also Arendt (1958), MacIntyre (1984), Ricoeur (1984), Carr (1986), Abbott (1992), Fehn et al. (1992), Rasmussen (1995) and Bal (1997).
62 See MacIntyre (1984:214-216).
63 See Mattingly (1991:237).
64 For examples of the influence on current organizational practices of traditions with long historical roots, see Putnam et al. (1993) and Flyvbjerg (1998), Chapter 8, "The *Longue Durée* of Power".
65 For a discussion of the problems incurred in moving beyond these dualisms, see Dreyfus & Rabinow (1982), and Thomas McCarthy's considerations on hermeneutics and structural analysis in his introduction to Jürgen Habermas's *The Theory of Communicative Action*, Vol. 1 (1984:xxvi-xxvii). See other works of interest on this problem, which, in my view, is one of the more challenging in phronetic organization research: Giddens (1982), Seung (1982) and Schmidt (1985).
66 See Bourdieu (1977:72).
67 See Bourdieu (1990:10).
68 See also Vaughan (1992:183).
69 See Vaughan (1992).
70 See Bellah, Madsen, Sullivan, Swidler & Tipton (1991:302).
71 See Vaughan (1992:182).
72 See Geertz (1973, 1977).
73 See Putnam, Leonardi & Nanetti (1993).
74 See Ferguson (1990).
75 See Herzfeld (1992).
76 See Tillyard (1994).
77 For more on the actor/structure issue, see Collins (1980), Giddens (1984), Coleman (1985), Bourdieu (1988), Fine (1988), Harrison (1989), Rosen (1989), Lévi-Strauss & Eribon (1991:102-104) and Sewell (1992).
78 For more on the relationship between the public sphere and science, see Bellah (1993).
79 See Bellah, Madsen, Sullivan, Swidler & Tipton (1985:307).
80 For an interpretation of *Habits of the Heart* as phronetic social science, see Flyvbjerg (2001:62-65).
81 See Nietzsche (1969b:119, §3.12).
82 See Nietzsche (1969c). See also Nietzsche (1968b:287, §530): "There are no isolated judgments! An isolated judgment is never 'true,' never knowledge; only in the connection and relation of many judgments is there any surety".
83 See Miller (1994:239-264).
84 See Latour (1996, 1999) and Rabinow (1996, 1999).
85 See Dean (1999).

86 See Miller & Rose (1997:1-36).
87 See Ewald (1986, 1996).
88 See Rabinow (1989) and Crush (1994:301-324).
89 See Donzelot (1979) and Harcourt (2001).
90 See Dean (1991) and Procacci (1993).
91 See Bartky (1990) and Minson (1993).
92 See Rose (1985, 1996).
93 See Leijon (1993, 1996), Brytting, de Geer & Silfverberg (1997), Johansson (1998) and Brytting (2001).
94 See Flyvbjerg (1998, 2001) and Flyvbjerg, Bruzelis & Rothengatter (2003). For more examples of relevant research, see Dean (1999:3-5) and Flyvbjerg (2001:162-65).

PUBLIC SOCIOLOGY

– Models of Relevance for the 21st Century

~

James B. Rule

A sociologist I know loves to pose a ticklish question: Imagine that our discipline was miraculously eliminated – wiped off the intellectual map, with departments disbanded, degrees expunged, learned associations somehow mysteriously vaporized. Would anyone notice the loss – my friend wonders – or feel the need to redress it? And if people did notice the gap and set out to fill it, what would they put in its place?

Of course, we sociologists would feel the loss at once – a loss of our livelihoods, of hard-won insights, of habits of inquiry that we have come to cherish. But what about the rest of the world – the 'end consumers', one might hope, of our insights and analyses? Would they feel themselves any the worse?

Fortunately for us, this question is mostly heuristic rather than practical. Sociology is an established discipline in most universities and in a variety of other settings – meaning that we do not have to reassert our intellectual *raison d'être* anew, for example, every fiscal year. But entertaining the question does force us to confront some issues basic to any consideration of 'public sociology'. To wit: How does sociology pay its keep? Granted that we insiders find all sorts of meaning and satisfaction in our activities, what difference do they make to those on the outside?

Asking such questions, it seems to me, nudges one to the conclusion that *any* vision of sociology has to have a public dimension, at least in some broad sense. A system for studying social life that yielded no insights useful to anyone outside its boundaries is ultimately unappealing to most people – including those outside our discipline who pay our bills.

True, one can conceive of any social science – or any other intellectual or aesthetic pursuit for that matter – as an exercise whose only criteria for success are ones that it sets strictly for itself. The economist Donald McCloskey once entertained just such a justification for his field, when he wrote: "In the flight of rockets the layman can see the marvel of physics, and in the applause of audiences the marvel of music. No one understands the marvel of economics who has not studied it with care".[1] Such a criterion is purely self-referential; that is, success is defined by standards strictly internal to a discipline. By definition, there would be no reason for anyone not initiated to the inherent satisfactions of such success to care about whether it occurs.

But McCloskey ends up rejecting this self-referential rationale in favour of a more 'public' economics. And as an empirical matter, I expect that few economists, and perhaps even fewer sociologists, are indifferent to the potential impact of their analyses on human affairs. Moreover, I want to argue that how we conceive of the larger social impact of our work has everything to do with the way we go about it – and that prevailing images of such impact in the eyes of the greater public shape the possibilities for any public sociology.

* * *

Among the institutions that shape our world, few are held in higher general esteem than science. Even debacles and embarrassments that might seem part and parcel of applied science – from pre-frontal lobotomies to nerve gas – are somehow perceived as results of science *gone wrong*, rather than integral to the noble enterprise of science itself.

A key reason for this resilient prestige, it seems to me, is the idea that science *sets its own ends* – that the terms of scientific success are somehow given in the idea of science, rather than dictated by the gritty preoccupations of human interest groups or interested parties. Perhaps it is this kind of thinking that makes it possible for disastrous social repercussions of science to be shrugged off as miscarriages of a basically noble enterprise. The idea is that 'Science' (with a capital 'S') tells the story of Nature (with a capital 'N'), and tells it dispassionately, without skew or distortion from partisan human interests.

Sociologists and philosophers of science today widely dispute this view of science – even as it applies to the hardest of the 'hard' sciences. But such doubts manifest themselves *a fortiori* with regard to the study of social life. Even those sociologists most attracted to natural science as a model for their work – to exact measurement, precise explanation or rigorous replication – would find it hard to deny that our analytical concerns arise from our interests in the world we study.

Thus, one might well conceive of a sociology, based on such a natural science model, as devoted to identifying, measuring and explaining regularities in social events or behaviour – relations between family background and personal success or between the organizational design of schools and their effectiveness in educating, to take two utterly standard examples. But not all the regularities that one might study are equally worthy of scholarly attention. A hypothetical analyst might develop an elegant and highly predictive quantitative model of the distribution of bottlecaps on city streets – that is, a multivariate analysis of what kinds of bottlecaps are found in which sorts of neighbourhoods, in what numbers and in what condition. But to win recognition for these feats, he or she would still need to provide some account of *why it mattered* to chart *these particular forms* of variation.

* * *

Perhaps even more than other theoretically-minded sociologists, I have long been fascinated with the complex rationales linking our practice of sociological inquiry and our aspirations for desirable consequences that we hope may ensue from our work. Few social scientists, I am convinced, remain unmoved by what I call *models of relevance* in their conduct of inquiry.[2]

By *models of relevance*, I mean our assumptions (perhaps not even consciously acknowledged) about how the insight likely to stem from our work is apt to be assimilated in some larger collective store of shared social understanding – and about how such knowledge, once assimilated, will promote or uphold some value we hold important. Models of relevance are accounts of how the understanding generated by our work actually moves specific intellectual 'consumers', and how such consumption contributes to making the world a better place. Models of relevance amount to intellectual 'connective tissue' that link sociologists' willingness to exert themselves in particular programs of social inquiry with those same sociologists' assessments of what forms of social amelioration are possible or desirable.

Models of relevance are thus conceptual hybrids, linking normative ideas of what constitutes desirable states of the social world with strictly analytical models of relations between ideas, action and social change. One part of any model of relevance is the identification of a *form* of knowledge that will represent the distinctive product of a particular line of intellectual work. Another is a kind of cause-effect model of how such knowledge will move specific actors. And a third part of any model of relevance, no less essential to the over-all idea, is value-based affirmation of specific forms of social intervention as desirable. Together, these elements provide a rationale as to how pursuit of a particular program of intellectual work is apt to make the world a better place. Thus, sociologists who study poverty often have their work guided by assumptions that understanding of the actual mechanisms creating and perpetuating poverty will trigger processes for alleviating it.

Note the pivotal role, for any model of relevance, of that category of actors identified as key 'consumers' of social inquiry. Hardly any engaged social scientists imagine that their ideas will be of uniform interest to any and all members of the public. Instead, the most distinctive and controversial differences among models of relevance turn on the crucial question of *who will be moved to action* by the insights arising from one's work.

To be sure, there is no *logical* reason why working social scientists need pay heed to any model of relevance at all. Dilettantism is always a possibility – in the form of the aforementioned sociology of bottlecap distributions or any other. I simply assert that such indifference to the larger social repercussions of one's work appears extraordinarily rare in our field. And for any social scientist interested in support and recognition from peers, funding agencies or academic institutions – which is to say, nearly all of us – open indifference to such larger value issues is apt to be highly counter-productive.

I certainly do not mean to suggest that all models of relevance embraced by working sociologists are subject to rigorous examination by those whose work they shape. Many, I suspect, are in effect 'deep structures' of intellectual life that their holders may not be able readily to articulate. Nevertheless, I suspect that even many sociologists who consider their work remote from practical application still entertain some inchoate notion as to how that work will support some crucial value. Historical sociologists who study long-dead peoples, for example, or ethnographers and linguists who study languages on the way to extinction, may see themselves as upholding the dignity or richness of ways of life that, they feel, deserve respectful attention, rather than cold indifference to their loss. Or a sociologist making a mathematical model of a bureaucracy, with no obvious practical implication, may at least feel that he or she is implicitly providing cautionary advice about the difficulty of changing such complex structures.

* * *

I should also emphasize that models of relevance differ vastly in the extent to which they are shared among communities of like-minded thinkers. Many sociologists, as I have said, seem moved by assumptions about the larger social role of their work that are largely private or shared only among closed circles. But other models of relevance attain almost iconic status. That is, they become master accounts of the larger purposes of social inquiry that inspire entire generations or groupings of sociologists to see themselves united in a worthy, common intellectual enterprise.

Consider Marxism – perhaps the most durably beguiling model of relevance ever formulated. It has proved its power to capture the sociological imagination and mobilize and give direction to the work of sociologists over many generations and across vastly different social settings. This power, I believe, derives from an ingenious juxtaposition of analytical and normative messages.

This juxtaposition begins with a distinctive identification of the conditions blocking movement to a better world – the conservative, self-serving, ultimately parasitic dominance of capitalists as an exploiting class. *If only* the retrograde grip of this group can be broken, Marxist thinking promises us, *then* vast human suffering and unproductive conflict can be short-circuited, and the way opened to full realization of human potential. In the new, bountiful world to follow the destruction of capitalism, exploitation of one class by another, the master template for social life throughout history, will be abolished. The task is simply to hasten this dramatic, qualitative break as much as possible.

But what role does *analysis* play in the overthrow of capitalism? Here the Marxist model of relevance is especially ingenious. The theory teaches that broad directions of consciousness and action are set down by actors' material position – including ideological falsifications and distractions generated by dominant capitalism. But if such processes of class domination in the realm of thought and action were totally determinate, there would be no rationale for the role of the analyst – a disaster from the point of view of people like ourselves, the intellectuals or the sociologists. Fortunately most varieties of Marxist thinking leave room for such a role. A few advanced thinkers, in these views, can transcend the intellectual constraints of their class positions so as to see the severe limits to human potential posed by the prevailing regime. By shedding light on crucial realities that others are unable to see, Marxist analysts can ultimately hasten the day when exploitation is finally swept away, and the master obstacles to enduring social betterment are eliminated.

Thus, all the elements required of any successful model of relevance can be found here – the specification of social processes leading to human betterment; the identification of a group or category of actors potentially willing and able to take such action; and a formula for production of just that form of knowledge destined to trigger such action.

Crucial to the appeal of this model is the pivotal role ascribed to the proletariat. The broad tenets of Marxist analysis, of course, cast the proletariat as an embattled class, struggling to gain understanding of its own true interests in juxtaposition to its historical class antagonist, the capitalists. But in the Marxist model of relevance, analysts – at least, the *right kind* of analysts – can support the *general* interest of humanity by supplying just the right kind of *partisan insight* to proletarian activists.[3] Thus, a view of relations between social inquiry and social betterment that dramatically puts thinkers on the side of the angels – or if not angels, then on the side of their secular counterpart, the class destined to end forever exploitation and all its attendant social miseries.

It would be hard to overemphasize the attractions of such a role to analysts in all eras and settings. Even the most seemingly obscure Marxist investigation, in this view, could theoretically help undermine class rule and hasten the realization of the best interests of humanity as a whole. As Karl Marx himself reminded us, in a famous line, the 11th Feuerbach thesis: the philosophers had sought only to understand the world; but the point is to change it.

Whether Marxist thinking has often had just the effects on social activism touted for it – and whether those effects deserve the enthusiasm held out for them – is not my concern for the moment. I simply invite you to consider the extraordinary appeal stemming from such a comprehensive rationale for a single program of social inquiry. This model, in its many historical variations, has mobilized the energies of countless analysts – and has focused the expectations of larger publics on the good results to be expected from the resulting efforts.

In fact, I doubt that our discipline could have gained the place it now holds in the academy and the larger world, without the moral impetus afforded by a handful of iconic models of relevance like Marx's. Sociology as a discipline, after all, is a historical creature; it came to exist under specific conditions, and in response to specific expectations. It is hard to believe that this or any other discipline could have won its established status – for example, as a subject for university study – without widespread conviction that it would support key public values. In fact, a few key figures like Marx managed to convince broad publics that their programs of inquiry would accomplish just that.

Marxism did not play much role in academic sociology during Marx's own lifetime – indeed, though his intent was a kind of public sociology, his public remained restricted to a relatively obscure world of revolutionary thought for some time after his death.

By contrast, Herbert Spencer, more or less Marx's contemporary, was an enormously successful public sociologist in his own lifetime – and bequeathed a distinctive model of relevance that continues to shape expectations of social inquiry down to the present. Especially in the United States, his view of competition and evolution as master processes of social life won him a following in the mid-19th century that hardly any public intellectual could aspire to today. As the American editor Henry Holt commented in his memoirs:

> Probably no other philosopher ever had such a vogue as Spencer had from about 1870 to 1890. Most preceding philosophers had presumably been mainly restricted to readers habitually given to the study of philosophy, but not only was Spencer considerably read and talked about by the whole intelligent world in England and America, but that world was wider than any that preceded it.[4]

Now *that* was a public sociologist!

The substance of Spencer's model of relevance is one-hundred eighty degrees opposite to Marx's. For Marx, the aim was to cut short the miseries generated by capitalism by furnishing insight into its fatal flaws. For Spencer and his many followers, the aim was to highlight and interpret the vast benefits of capitalism, competition and markets – and by demonstrating the ultimate beneficence of these forces, to dissuade those tempted to kill the goose producing the golden eggs of economic growth and social innovation. The intellectual 'consumers' targeted by Marx's thinking were the proletariat and their immediate allies. For Spencer and his followers, the key intended consumers were, one might argue, public figures and policy-makers intelligent enough to absorb the message that state intervention and interference with market processes could only bring about stagnation.

In some sense, the implications for human action yielded by the kind of insight Spencer favoured were largely negative – messages as to what things *not* to do, in order to realize the benefits of competition and markets. But like Marx's vision, Spencer's offered a broad account of the indispensable role that could (and should) be played by a particular line of social inquiry, in upholding values ultimately shared by humanity in the broadest sense.

Another model of relevance from the late 19th century that surely played a major role in securing public recognition for sociology was Émile Durkheim's. Here we confront a particularly close identification between the fortunes of the discipline and that of the individual. Durkheim, of course, aspired to be the first professor of sociology in France, but to do this he had to establish both the analytical distinctness of the discipline and the public role it was to play. He responded with his own distinctive vision – embodying both substantive differences from both Marx and Spencer on the workings of early capitalism and of the larger social payoffs to be expected from sociological analysis. In all these efforts, let us note, he vigorously promoted his own particular brand of public sociology, well before the term had a name.

The basis of Durkheim's appeal was a vision of societies as *moral organisms* – systems whose constituent institutions and individuals *needed* one another and required direction from a common moral authority. Atomistic thinkers like Spencer, Durkheim held, could not see the forest of social life for the trees of pleasure-maximizing individuals. Revolutionary thinkers like Marx, for their part, failed to grasp the ultimate moral interdependence of different elements of populations. Only by recognizing the reality of any viable society as a moral organism could sociologists play the public role that Durkheim staked out for them – that of *physicians of society*, specialists in providing advice as to how the body social can best be strengthened and improved.

Thus, another distinct model of relevance with its characteristic definitions of the forms of insight most required to support key social values; identification of actors most likely to act on such insight (progressive policy-makers and community leaders, perhaps); and the forms of action and policy likely to ensue from their insights.

One could equally well consider additional thinkers who have provided such iconic master visions of the role of sociological analysis in social betterment. Gunnar Myrdal and C. Wright Mills are 20th century figures who come to mind. Particularly during the years of ferment and protest in western universities in the 1960s and 1970s, ideas deriving from Mills and his intellectual allies had a tremendously galvanizing effect. These ideas helped draw an entire generation into sociology – in the process, changing the theoretical landscape drastically. And at the same time, the intellectual movement triggered by Mills changed expectations outside our field as to what sociologists could be expected to contribute.

* * *

But in the generation since those heady times – in their U.S. manifestation, I like to call them the 'great American cultural revolution' – I discern a sea change. I can no longer identify any compelling model of relevance moving social scientists, either in my own country or abroad, that has anything like the influence of ideas like Mills's – or like Durkheim's, Marx's or Spencer's – though some qualification is necessary in the latter case.

This is not to say that sociologists have stopped caring about the larger value relevance of their work – or that the rest of the world has stopped expecting value-relevant work from us. I have already suggested that I consider it almost constitutionally impossible for most of us *not* to entertain some such hopes and expectations for larger good consequences from our work, no matter how privately or how tentatively.

What I do notice is a secular decline in the influence of what I see as compelling *master models* – models like those cited above, purporting to identify a single Archimedean lever for social betterment, and that accordingly can mobilize the efforts of many or all sociologists. Working sociologists simply seem much less likely to perceive themselves as joining broad categories of other researchers in a single, master process of ameliorative social change.

Why should this be? Perhaps one answer has to do with what might be called the intellectual immune reactions built up through exercise of our own critical faculties. Having seen the expected gains touted by a number of master models short-circuited by history, we perhaps turn a more critical eye to future claims of a similar sort.

Think of Durkheim's model of relevance – and especially of the extraordinary claims it entailed for the public authority of sociological advice. Durkheim actually believed that the expertise of the sociologists qualified them to issue authoritative advice on all social affairs, including matters of politics, public morality and social policy. As I have argued elsewhere, such claims derive from a tradition of visions going back at least to the founders of our discipline, Saint Simon and Auguste Comte – a tradition of what I regard as quasi-religious faith that insights derived from social science should ultimately trump the sordid play of political forces in human affairs.[5]

But it is hard to credit those claims today – at least in the extreme form made by Durkheim. Who now believes, either inside or outside of sociology, that the advice of our profession on all matters of social practice can (even in principle) be as dispassionate, as a-political, as medical advice? No one could consistently do so, it seems to me, if only because of the evident fact that sociologists – and well-informed, widely-respected, accomplished ones, at that – end up embracing such a vast variety of political positions.

True, sociologists generally gravitate to the left side of the political spectrum. But there are many distinguished exceptions to this generalization. And among those on the left, the variety of positions, even conflicting positions, on the implications of sociological insight for social practice remains vast. It is simply very difficult to claim, in light of manifest empirical evidence, that the insight deriving from sociological analysis generates a unique and unambiguous set of directions for action on value-charged issues. If the sociologist is indeed to be an authoritative 'physician of society' a la Durkheim, in other words, why do we have so many often contradictory treatment plans?

I hardly mean to suggest that Durkheim's ideas on the role of sociological advice in the improvement of social relations have lost all influence. Indeed, I suspect that some version of them – probably many versions – shape the thinking of many of today's working sociologists, as I suppose that they do my own. Many of us proceed with our work on a rather vague assumption that its implications for a 'healthier' society will somehow be apparent to most alert observers – or at least to some sort of community of policy makers open to objectively 'good ideas' for social change.

But if we are honest, we have to confess skepticism that good ideas are so unambiguously good as to be assured of implementation. *Contra* Durkheim, visions of what constitutes a 'healthy' society are all but infinitely varied, and those variations have everything to do with contending political visions. Insights that appear as life-giving and indispensable steps toward a better society from one point of view are assured of no such reception elsewhere. Proposals for special assistance to disadvantaged families, for example, will appear to some commentators, and some members of the public, as rewards for irresponsible or improvident family behaviour – as indeed, a reincarnated Spencer would bracket them. Thus, when today's working social scientists generate insight intended to point the way to 'better' social arrangements, they must do without the serene certainty implied in Durkheim's vision that sociological insight should be seen as transcending politics. Durkheim's religion, one might say, has shattered into a multiplicity of sects.

Today, among all models of relevance issuing from the 19th-century roots of sociology, only those derived from Spencer seem to have retained the ability to inspire historical confidence among their adherents. The idea that markets and competition represent master processes for the realization of key social values continues to hold the imagination of broad sectors of the global public. These views are obviously stronger in economics and, probably, political science than in sociology. But for some sociologists, the notion holds sway that applying the wisdom of market relations to every aspect of social life represents a royal road to social betterment. A major statement in this tradition is the late James Coleman's monumental *Foundations of Social Theory* (1989).

This model of relevance has a kind of political twin – the liberal triumphalism emanating from governing circles in Washington D.C. since the collapse of the Soviet Union. According to this view, those events left the world with a single viable set of political principles – notably, some version of American democracy. The role for the analysis implied here is, perhaps, simply to demonstrate the futility of any search for alternative. In its most extreme form, this line of thinking involves a kind of new historicism, in Karl Popper's sense of dangerous moral certainty that one knows the ultimate directions of history. Like the Marxist version of historicism, this vision has moved some thinkers to support highly destructive actions, confident that the ultimate triumph of democracy will balance some horrific moral equation.

* * *

Perhaps not everyone will share my perception that versions of Spencer's model of relevance, extolling the role of markets and competition, retain influence among 21st century sociologists. But whether or not this is true, I would still hold that master models of relevance – those that simultaneously command the imaginations of large numbers of working sociologists – are waning in influence. One could say that sociology is experiencing what another of our famous intellectual ancestors might have termed the 'disenchantment of the world' in these respects. Confident, widely-shared visions of widespread social improvement resulting from specific forms of sociological practice – like those of Mills in the 1960's or those of Marx at many points – appear scarcer and less influential today.

One reason for this, I have posited, may simply be that we feel that 'we've been there'. The more we see sweeping visions of social change as orchestrated by sociological ideas confounded in the historical event, perhaps the harder it is to sustain such belief in further models of relevance. But I suspect that an even more important reason has to do with changes in our shared view of the future *in general*. When I say *our* view of the future, I do not just mean that of sociologists, but views current among thoughtful observers around the world. We simply do not share the kind of simplified, coherent map of what is next for humanity that furnished the intellectual environment for many earlier models of relevance.

Certainly Spencer, Durkheim and Marx were all confronting – and concomitantly, shaping – widely shared views of *progress*. That is, people in their times shared perceptions of a world on the way to becoming more prosperous, more subject to innovation or simply more advanced in the direction of some long-term evolutionary model. Obviously, such expectations came in many different forms. But all involved a widespread sense that the world was moving in a particular direction – leaving the way open for sociologists to specify that direction and to posit a role for sociological insight in it.

I do not believe that the world has any such equivalent master narrative of its own future, as of the beginning of the 21st century. This is not because public intellectuals, or any others, do not speculate on the matter – on the contrary. But we simply do not seem to agree which way things are headed. Or to the extent that we do agree, we do not see a single, catalytic role for social science advice in planning the trip.

Of course, history will continue, even though educated opinion cannot agree on a single characterization of the direction. And such lack of agreement notwithstanding, observers do agree on a handful of processes all but certain to bulk large in our immediate global future.

One of these is the confrontation between the world's prosperous liberal democracies in the West and militant Islam. No sociologist, no matter how repelled by the cruel and violent manifestations of this collision, can avoid being fascinated by this historic tension. Fortunately, many good minds are focusing attention on precisely these dynamics – and on other, parallel conflicts between liberal values and anti-modern forces at work around the world. But I do not think that sociological inquiry into these crucial processes is at all likely to partake of, or to inspire, any single, influential model of relevance.

The reason for this, it seems to me, is that no one can see a distinctive form of knowledge arising from sociological investigation that would plausibly help improve the situation in a single, distinctive way. By this I hardly mean to deny that the results of our inquiries can be useful. I simply mean that there seems no single, positive form of social change in sight that could be expected to result from the influence of sociological inquiry – nothing comparable to the definitive end to exploitation in history that inspired Marxist analysts as the ultimate fruit of their endeavours. One reason for this is that we simply do not agree on any shared scenario for the outcome of the conflicts between radical Islam and the West. Another is that the outcomes of this conflict, for better or for worse, do not seem susceptible to influence in any one, predictable, positive direction through sociological understanding.

Next, consider a second salient, impending historical change that is widely expected over the coming decades: developments having to do with humanity's troubled relationship with the natural environment. Nearly everyone agrees that this complex of challenges – including pollution, resource depletion, climate change, mass extinctions and related matters – are all but certain to make the life of the next generation sharply different from our own. In contrast to the late 19th and early 20th century faith in progress, few if any expectations of these developments foresee change for the better. The expected changes, whatever their exact form, will surely involve new constraints on human experience – ranging from reduced living standards to higher mortality rates from certain diseases to sharpened conflicts over scarce resources.

Here, too, we can be glad that many sociologists and other social scientists are directing their attention to these developments. But as with Islamic radicalism, this intellectual ferment does not seem to partake in or support any single model of relevance – nor does it seem likely to generate one. Notwithstanding intense debate and investigation, no consensus scenario for social change in the face of environmental uncertainties over the coming decades has emerged. What insults to the environment will exact the greatest price? What constraints on our consumption habits or freedom of action will we most likely experience first, and most acutely? Will alternative sources of energy emerge, so as to leave current ways of life recognizable? How will global and national patterns of governance be shaped by these developments? No one has, to my knowledge, succeeded in spinning answers to questions like these into a master narrative or iconic model of relevance for the coming decades – let alone found room for a particular form of sociological insight to shape the unfolding of such a narrative.

We do not know what forms of sociological insight will matter in the shaping the outcome of these developments. We do not agree what parties could or should act on any sociological insight that might be offered. And, in fact, we probably do not readily agree on what outcomes to these crises would be most desirable. None of this reflects lack of good ideas or intentions emanating from sociological students of environmental change. I simply note that no single, widely-convincing model has emerged of where we are going, or of what role sociological inquiry might play in charting our course.

One might make generalizations like these about countless other major social trends and developments shaping the world today – secularization, for example, or the evolution of the family, or the future of the nation-state. I can think of no such broad form of social change that has been cast in the sort of narrative that makes room for the ascendance of a master sociological model of relevance.

Please do not interpret these words as some 21st century version of an 'end of ideology' thesis – the notion that classic political programs have lost, or should lose, their abilities to move us, and that sociology accordingly has no role to play in upholding or realizing political values. Most emphatically, I am not suggesting that there are no meaningful alternatives or compelling differences among visions for change in any of these respects. On the contrary, I believe that such visions of ameliorative change are numerous and significant. Some sociologists see themselves as engaged in inquiry aimed at making state institutions more effective, for example, whereas others seek insight aimed at encouraging attenuation of state power. One could extend such examples to virtually any corner of our field. In a way, this situation is not so unusual in the history of our field: we are sleeping in the same institutional bed with one another, but we are dreaming different dreams. My point is simply that, in contrast to earlier periods in our discipline's history, the multiplicity of dreams is at least as great as it has ever been.

Could this change? Most certainly. Charismatic transformations of consciousness are always possible. Perhaps a new moral vision of future events will emerge – implying a new, missionary role for sociological insight. One can imagine the rise of a radical new mindset, for example, aimed at renunciation of 'high' technology in all of its forms, and dedicated to developing new types of social organization consistent with such renunciation. One might also posit that many social scientists might be swept up in such a movement, dedicating their analytical resources to efforts to demonstrate its feasibility and attractiveness. Such involvement would, of course, imply the rise of an influential new model of relevance to guide such work. Certainly, such a new direction in social evolution could represent one plausible response to environmental shocks and to frustrations with the rigidities of states as ways of organizing our governance.

But does such a development strike me as very likely? No. I simply sense little intellectual enthusiasm, as of 2007/2008, for certainty as to any unique step as necessary to reverse the world's ills – nor confidence as to how some particular form of social inquiry might push such change in a particular direction. And what I have called iconic models of relevance, those with the power to unite large numbers of analysts in what they define as a shared moral enterprise, requires a big dose of certainty.

Instead the visions of social change that animate our work are heterogeneous and sometimes even mutually contradictory. Some students of educational institutions, for example, pursue their work in hopes of drawing attention to promising new approaches to school administration or more meaningful evaluation of student performance. Students of economic growth devote themselves to perfecting new measures of prosperity in hopes of encouraging planners to define the goals of their efforts more broadly. Students of hierarchy in organizations struggle to identify new openings for improved flexibility in work arrangements. And on and on.

Worthy projects all, informed by models of relevance that have much to recommend them. But not apocalyptic. If I am right, relatively few sociologists in the immediate future will orient their inquiries to providing support for sweeping forms of transformation for entire social systems. Instead of thinking of ourselves as involved in a single concerted effort to realize a comprehensive model of social change, we will orient our work to promoting an array of more specific good results in specific settings.

* * *

And so, if our discipline were indeed somehow magically eliminated, the losses would be considerable. Lost would be a multiplicity of ideas for improving specific areas of social life – including a number that are neither consistent with current practice nor with one another. It is a good thing that we have this multiplicity, as it represents a bountiful source of critical reflection on public thinking about all social topics.

I sometimes think that the existence of social science, and not least sociology, as an institution represents the social equivalent of diversity in the human gene pool – or the diversity of species in the world eco-system. Even if our ideas are not currently embodied in practice, the social world is better off that they exist, even latently, as a source of alternative directions. As such, they represent a public resource, even if they do not always point with a single voice toward a single form of social change.

NOTES

1. Donald N. McCloskey (1985): *The Rhetoric of Economics*. Madison, WI: University of Wisconsin Press, p. xix.
2. See James B. Rule (1978): "Models of Relevance: The Social Effects of Sociology". *American Journal of Sociology*, 84 (1):78-98.
3. Some schools of Marxism, disappointed at the failure of the proletariat to rise to its historic mission, designate other categories of actors as consumers of their special insights. For the Frankfurt School, for example, those stand-ins for the industrial proletariat were a more diffuse category of critical thinkers, designated in the first instance as the ones destined act on the insights of Marxist analysis.
4. Quoted in Richard Hofstadter (1944): *Social Darwinism in American Thought: 1860-1915*. Philadelphia, PA, University of Pennsylvania Press, p. 21.
5. James Rule & Yasemin Besen (forthcoming): "The Once and Future Information Society". *Theory and Society*.

PLURALISM AND CRITIQUE
– Public Sociology versus Academic Sociology

~

Henrik Dahl

INTRODUCTION

This is an entirely subjective tribute to pure sociology, given by a practical sociologist on the occasion of the tenth anniversary of the Sociology Program at Aalborg University. Having worked as a practical sociologist for many years, I have found pure sociology extremely valuable and useful. I would not have missed recent developments in pure sociology for anything, as they have been a great inspiration in my everyday professional life.

But having been a frequent visitor to the world of pure sociology without ever being truly enculturated as a permanent, legal resident or citizen, I have also wondered about many things: the frequent lack of social graces among those who study the social; the aggression towards deviant colleagues – even among the champions of tolerance in the general society, and the way care for the lot of the ordinary citizen is usually expressed in language and concepts entirely un-intelligible by the common man. It is definitely true, as one colleague jokingly told me once: If you mix a mobster with a sociologist, you get an offer you cannot understand.

None of the following was written to put down pure sociology. Only as an attempt by a practical sociologist to understand its special features and to point out where, in all modesty, pure sociology could perhaps learn from or be inspired by practical sociology.

ON THE DISTINCTION AND THE DISAGREEMENTS BETWEEN PURE AND PRACTICAL SOCIOLOGY

For most of my post-university career, which began when I quit the Roskilde University as an assistant professor in 1994 to become head of research and development at ACNielsen, I have had to use whatever I was taught at the university in the way of theories and methodologies as a skill. That is: I have had to consider sociology as an ability to *do* something practical or perhaps more accurately: to consider sociology as the foundation for a number of practical abilities, I have developed into a sort of profession, the main elements of which have been designing empirical studies, giving advice to those who commissioned the studies, writing books for the general public and commenting on social phenomena in the media.

The distinction between pure knowledge and practical skill may seem trivial, but is not. When receiving them, my university degrees immediately gave me the feeling I knew everything. But I soon came to realize that knowing something is no proof one is able to do anything. I am tempted to say 'on the contrary', because of encounters with quite a few people, who were extremely knowledgeable, but hardly able to perform any practical task at all. But I hesitate, because I can also think of knowledgeable people who were, at the same time, very skilful – sometimes even within the field in which they were knowledgeable. So I suppose the best thing to say is that there is no necessary relationship between knowledge and skills.

Having tried out life both as a pure and a practical academic, it is relevant to compare the two forms of life and ask: what is the difference? In my personal experience, the main difference is that being a practical academic raises questions of risk and responsibility, or in short: consequences, which are very different from the problems the pure academic has to deal with. Applying a skill is equivalent to *doing something* in a very fundamental way that for instance discussing the merits of two different theories or the most appropriate interpretation of some phenomenon is not. Discussing interpretations, or even deciding that one is better than another, does not involve *responsibility* the same way it does to investigate some social phenomenon and make recommendations on this background. If you recommend something, in your capacity as a professional, and it results in failure or disaster, you may be held legally responsible for your actions. And even in the cases where no lawsuit is taken out against you, you could be morally responsible – in the eyes of yourself or others, or even both.

The pure academics seem to have a different relationship to responsibility. If you favour a completely foolish theory, and for some time are able to win over the academic community for your illusions, you will suffer no consequences that are even remotely reminiscent of the ones legal responsibility may have. No legal process. No jail sentence. No fine. No public disgrace. As long as you stay within academia and stick to pure theory, you can walk away from even the worst academic disasters with your head held high and are under no obligation to display the slightest remorse for wasting a generation of students or two for your own ambitions.

I am not advocating that pure academics who, for instance, promote bad theories in spite of convincing evidence that they are in fact bad, should be held legally responsible. Inside the realm of academia we need boldness and a willingness to run risks. Such an attitude is crucial for anybody who wants to advance our knowledge and understanding beyond the existing frontiers, and in return for the willingness to take risks, the academic community should grant a certain degree of immunity to those who do, but whose enterprises fail. If the system did not work that way, our knowledge and understanding would never improve, or only improve much slower than it had to.

Practical academics need to be much more cautious. Sociologists are rarely able to inflict the same degree of harm on others as are, for instance, surgeons, engineers or jurists. If they fail, people may be killed or put in extremely unpleasant circumstances because of their failure. But even practical sociologists have to understand and accept the risk that they may make the lives of others extremely miserable. For instance, if they design social programs that do not work or somehow misfire; if they design organizations that are unfit for anybody to work in or if money and jobs are lost as a result of their ill advice.

Faced with the prospect of creating such degrees of harm (and with the resulting risk of litigation or criminal charges), practical academics need to think up an appropriate response. One very practical response is, of course, insurance and in many cases insurance is mandatory for anybody joining a profession. But whether you take precautions because they are necessary for obtaining insurance or you just take them anyway, they are pretty much the same:

- The profession may be joined only by certified practitioners.
- Professional activities may never fall below certain standards as regards processes, procedures, concepts, equipment and quality control.
- All professional activities should be carried out with the utmost care and attention to the well-being of others.
- All unnecessary risks should be avoided at all time.

I have always found it intriguing that by trying to minimize the risk of harming others, you tend to become what would in many parts of academia be construed as very old-fashioned and 'positivistic'. Whether you think you are a positivist or not, the desire not to expose others to unnecessary risks almost compels the practical academic to ask questions like: "what is the best knowledge available about this problem?", "what is the best theory guiding my search for data or my interpretation of data?", "how can I be sure my data do not deceive me?", etc.

It would be the easiest thing in the world to give polemical responses to this state of affairs. "Modern views of (social) science are just for the irresponsible". Or: "Responsibility does for (social) science what real estate does for politics: no matter how wild your ideas used to be, they instil common sense in you immediately". But this type of response would only create a division between pure and practical social science I think is entirely uncalled for. As a practical social scientist, it is imperative that I know what is going on in academia as far as new theories and methods are concerned. For if I did not constantly monitor the relevant parts of academia, I would not be practicing my profession properly. So from the point of view of practical sociology, I find it the case that we cannot do without institutions like the university, whose primary task (I suppose) it is to propose new theories and methods and to critically assess them.

But what about practical sociology, as it is perceived from the point of view of pure sociology? To be quite honest, I think the relationship is much more strained than it is from the opposite point of view. I have personally met quite a few pure sociologists who dismissed the results from practical sociology on the grounds that they had been obtained as a means to reach practical goals, or because money had been paid to commission a study. I simply fail to see why practical ends or the transfer of money for a contract to carry out a certain study necessarily and causally would result in flawed research. I can easily see why that kind of research could end up being biased, as I can see why research sponsored by tax-money and commissioned by government institutions in order to improve social engineering could end up biased. The main reason, as far as I can tell, is the same reason that endangers the validity of all research: it is carried out by human beings.

But it is very hard to understand the implicit logic in the proposition that contracts paid with capitalist money should pose a bigger threat to the validity of social science than contracts paid with tax-money, or that private organizations would be more prone to exert undue pressure upon researchers than public organizations would. In fact, from the point of view of Weberian or even Luhmannian sociology, the hypothesis would be just the opposite: private organizations are more likely to be rational than public organizations. Therefore, they are less likely to put researchers under forms of pressure that will result in irrationality such as, for instance, deliberate bias.

On the Nature of the Disagreement between Pure and Practical Sociologists

As I write this, I have been a sociologist for slightly more than twenty years. In the course of those twenty years, I have noticed that when sociologists are brought together in larger numbers, they almost inevitably begin to question their professional identity, and quite often this debate turns into regular quarrels.

Underlying a large number of sociological disagreements is probably a sort of embarrassment. It is very hard to define basic, sociological concepts (one may think of, for instance, 'modernity' or 'solidarity'). And even in those cases where a sub-community inside the general, sociological community agrees to some definition, it is usually next to impossible to measure, for instance, modernity or solidarity.

From the point of view of practical sociology, I would say that very strong disagreements over things that are ill-defined and hard to measure, are typical examples of what happens in the case when there is no 'pragmatic option'. Let me explain. Among medical doctors, there is no generally agreed-upon definition of such basic concepts as 'health' or 'sickness'. But most medical doctors do not worry about this. Or better, I believe: they have found more productive ways than have the pure sociologists of dealing with the troubling fact that they cannot define the basic concepts underlying their professional endeavour – which I take, for medical doctors, to be the restoring of the health of sick people. Instead of worrying about metaphysical questions that may never find a satisfactory answer, doctors have taught themselves to live with operational definitions. They accept the definitions of, say, the WHO and proceed to go about their daily business without too much metaphysical concern.

One important difference between medical doctors and pure sociologists is that most medical doctors have the pragmatic option of including their results when assessing the problems of metaphysical uncertainty. This is very difficult for the pure sociologists. Due to the fact that they possess nothing that may be counted as 'results', the weight of metaphysical uncertainty is much more likely to be perceived as unbearable.

In my personal experience, disagreement is much stronger when pure sociologists are involved in debates with other pure sociologists or with practical sociologists than it is when similar social groups debate. I have personally witnessed levels of aggression I found comparable only to disagreement about schismatic religious differences inside hardcore or esoteric religious communities. Therefore, I shall try to argue that when pure sociologists are involved, the level of tension has a tendency to rise to the level of tension among people divided by schismatic differences for reasons that all boil down to the same: the lack of a pragmatic option among those who have decided to forsake interaction with the ordinary world.

Consider the difference between medical doctors and pure sociologists in terms of handling metaphysical uncertainty. Immediately, one important element comes to mind. In the case of doctors, the lack of metaphysical certainty is counterbalanced by two factors: (a) the prevailing consensus in the medical profession that medicine has made great, scientific progress over the past 150 years, and (b) the support enjoyed by the medical profession from the general public.

Pure sociologists have nothing akin to these counterbalancing forces. As a community, they hardly agree on anything. Not even the direction in which one or more steps would count as a success. And there is no general population anxiously waiting for pure sociologists to bring release from pain or premature death. If their activities improve the conditions of the general population at all, it is hardly ever noticed by it.

At this point, a pure sociologist could point out that my comparison with medicine is not at all fair. It is common knowledge that the sciences, the humanities and the social sciences are, epistemologically speaking, too different to be compared. Scientific curiosity is properly satisfied by *explanations*. Humanistic curiosity is properly satisfied by *interpretations* and social scientific curiosity by *interpretive explanations*. Most of us therefore agree that, for instance, pursuing the social sciences or the humanities in a nomothetical spirit or pursuing the sciences in an ideographical spirit constitute undesirable hybrids, destined to yield only empty and meaningless results.

In general, I am a strong supporter of the neo-Kantian project of extending the program of the *Critique of Pure Reason* to comprise the analysis of the limits of possible and meaningful knowledge in all intellectual fields – if for no other reason, then because the Kantian approach would allow the already over-worked sociologist, pure or practical, to discard entire *families* of propositions if they fell outside the limits of possible and meaningful knowledge.

But a word of caution against over-emphasis on the neo-Kantian project is necessary. It is far more sketchy than Immanuel Kant's own project (which gained in clarity, but perhaps lost in scope by generally using Newtonian physics as the paradigm for science in general), and does not take the variations inside the broad categories of 'the sciences', 'the humanities' and 'the social sciences' into due consideration. To illustrate the sketchiness of the general, neo-Kantian distinctions: even though medicine is, on the whole, a science, it cannot disregard problems of interpretation (for instance: what is the difference and the relation between feeling and being sick?) or social construction (for instance: is pregnancy and child-birth 'sickness' or not?). Therefore, medicine must necessarily concern itself with both explanations (what causes cancer?), interpretations (what do people mean when they say they are un-well?) and interpretive explanations (why is pregnancy sometimes and in some places considered to be an abnormal medical condition, and at other times and in other places the opposite?). Or to give another example: even though linguistics and the study of individual languages are usually institutionalized in universities with the humanities, a number of grammatical and, not least, phonetic observations (for instance: the Latin-Germanic p-f transformation) have a nature that lends itself much more readily and sensibly to explanation of the covering law-type than to interpretation.

As my line of reasoning and my examples show, a construction of the neo-Kantian project that implies a *ban* on, for instance, interpretation in the sciences or the establishing of laws in the humanities can very clearly be shown to be extremely counter-productive. Therefore, I find it hard to imagine that anything useful could be gained from a ban on explanation or pure interpretation in the social sciences – and, as a further consequence, it is quite reasonable and fair to make comparisons across neo-Kantian borders to discuss problems and challenges of individual (social) sciences.

As I stated earlier, metaphysical uncertainty may be aggravated by the lack of a pragmatic option or alleviated by its presence. Let me apply this observation to pure sociologists. Contrary to dentists and engineers, and even people with degrees in English and German, pure sociologists usually do not master a craft and never experience the joy of being truly wanted or in high demand. This makes them more similar to the elderly spinster aunts and uncles invited to family functions by dutiful relatives, than it makes them to the truly interesting people you want to see, because you can easily imagine what they could do for you – and what you would like to do with them. Pure sociologists do not know anything that is not contested or contradicted by other pure sociologists. Just a few have skills others really wish they had themselves, and a similarly small number is – unlike doctors, dentists, engineers, accountants, lawyers, architects or Spanish teachers – able to rid ordinary people of problems that seriously bug them. If pure sociologists could only give peoples' feelings or experiences back to them in words they had never heard before, but made them truly understand the human condition – like writers do – there would be a role in ordinary society for pure sociologists. But the prose of most pure sociologists is denser than the Amazon jungle, and for that reason it will never liberate anybody's feelings or thoughts.

But even though pure sociologists like to think otherwise, they are just people. And as we know from Pierre Bourdieu, the most common response of people, who are apparently stuck in some situation, to the depressing fact that they seem to be stuck, is not to change the situation they have wound up in, but to make a virtue out of necessity.

So, instead of asking: how could we possibly make ourselves sufficiently relevant to the general community or the public not to have to worry about the metaphysical questions we can never answer, pure sociologists have opted for another solution: they have decided that it is much nobler to be consumed by questions about metaphysics and identity, than it is to build a social scientific community bound by rules similar to those that bind other intellectual communities, or than it is to develop skills that will be sought after in the wider society.

This type of social organization, characterized by withdrawal from the world, a reluctance to perform productive work, a consequent dependence on revenue from taxation, and finally a focus on spiritual matters, is somewhat reminiscent of monastic orders.

And maybe it also explains why disagreements involving pure sociologists often reach the tension and the heights of religious disagreement, as mentioned above.

Why Pure Sociology Should Consider Going Back to Common Standards of Criticism

Of course, the tensions inside pure sociology would not exist if there were no schisms – if there were not, as is the case today, a number of sociologies, but only one true and unified sociology. But I think it would be a waste of time to sit back and wait for the day of unified sociology to come, as it probably never will. Experience so far has taught us that any attempt to force sociology into conformity with one scientific paradigm is bound to fail. Regardless of what paradigm or school of thought local power groups (for instance heads of departments or journal editors) would want sociology to conform to, dissent will soon emerge – even within the jurisdiction of the power group in question. In this respect, George Ritzer's classical description of sociology as a 'multi-paradigm science' is as fitting as ever.

Therefore, pure sociology today is in a complicated state. Exhausted from years and years of civil war, the pure sociologists have opted for their own version of the Treaty of Westphalia, which ended thirty years of war by affirming and consolidating the principle of *cuius regio, eius religio*. The local ruler decides, without interference from the outside, what is to be the official religion. On the surface, this has created a pluralistic peace in the world of pure sociology. Those who serve Master A do sociology the way he thinks is right. Those who serve Master B do it the way she thinks. And according to the modified principle of *cuius regio, eius religio*, nobody under A's jurisdiction can say anything to anybody under B's – and vice versa.

In the world of practical sociology, people still criticize one another professionally by applying old-fashioned principles of (social) science. Are the methods reliable? Are the results valid? Are there any internal contradictions? And what about correspondence with established knowledge? The sort of fallibilistic and positivistic nonsense no pure sociologist believes in any more, but which the practical sociologist is too scared by the risk of negative practical consequences not to believe in.

Most practical sociologists know that empirical sociology is more akin to physical experiments than it is to physical measurements: even though it is hard, in any strict sense, to measure anything, you can still get important, empirical input for your understanding of the social world by letting something happen and study the outcome carefully. They also know that theoretical choices are much more a matter of point of view than a matter of truth versus falsehood. So in many ways, they are in line with the pure sociologists.

The real issue between pure and practical sociology remains the question of risk: you must be reasonably certain, in order not to expose others to unnecessary risk, that you have used the most relevant theories and the best methods, and that you have done so skilfully. Therefore, you lapse back, as a practical sociologist, to ways of thinking often considered old-fashioned by pure sociologists.

What all this boils down to is the following: the real difference between pure and practical sociology is a vast difference in the understanding of the institution of 'critique'.

To save pure sociology form a devastating civil war, it has been necessary to introduce the idea of pluralism: "I'm okay stating that A is the case, and you're okay stating non-A is the case. So, since we belong to different paradigms and both feel okay, all is well". Of course, nobody *really* believes this, as it presents an outrage to any logical animal. But having given up common standards of critique, because they are old-fashioned fallibilism and positivism, pure sociologists now tend to talk about the work of other sociologists in purely subjective terms: "This doesn't work, because I disagree politically". "That doesn't work, because I disagree morally". "And this has to be rejected because it was written by somebody I know for sure is an idiot". To my ears, this is the sound of professional *critique* by pure sociologists today, because they no longer seem to believe in shared, (social) scientific values allowing rational criticism across paradigms.

Striking a balance between pluralism and critique is, as far as I can see, the real challenge of pure sociology today. The pluralism of modern, pure sociology has extremely positive sides, inasmuch as it vitalizes the entire field of sociology tremendously. But it also has very negative sides: the whole idea that anything goes stands in the way of true, (social) scientific progress, because it prevents (social) science from doing what anything that calls itself a science must ultimately do: get rid of bad ideas by replacing them with good ones. It is hard to imagine how anybody would, in the long run, benefit from a sociology defined by conforming to some orthodoxy – no matter what kind of orthodoxy one imagined. On the other hand, it is also hard to imagine how anybody would benefit from a sociology that no longer subscribed to any notion of scientific progress. At any rate: should the pure sociologists decide among themselves that there is no such thing as scientific progress any more, I can assure everybody that the practical sociologists would test and check the various propositions made by pure sociologists anyway. Why? Because we need to rank them from best to worst in order to safely apply them to problems in the ordinary world.

Given the history of pure sociology, I understand why it has ended up in pluralism. But if the ultimate goal of talking about propositions and knowledge is no longer to separate the valid from the invalid, we are not loyal to the concept of (social) science anymore. We could be doing lots of meaningful things: having a conversation, sharing subjective points of view to create a psychological bond or expressing beliefs, religious or otherwise. These pursuits are quite all right, and I have no objections to them whatsoever – but I cannot see how they could qualify as 'science'.

As I have already said: practical sociology needs pure sociology. But in many ways, pure sociology needs practical sociology as well, because it needs to reconstruct the institution of *critique* without starting new religious wars. Perhaps a very simple start would be to establish as a premise, that you cannot criticize a colleague for betraying *my* values – only for betraying his or her own values, or for betraying our common values. This is the way practical sociology has worked for many years: criticizing colleagues for betraying their own values in the sense of not delivering what they promised to deliver, or for betraying common values of logical and sound reasoning. This has worked very well for us in minimizing the risk of our profession. Maybe it would also work well for the pure sociologists in trying to figure out that sociological propositions are to be believed in some or all circumstances, and what propositions simply do not make any sense.

THE MEDIA AS PUBLIC
– The Appearance of Sociology in the Media Environment

~

Keith Tester

> "Repressive intolerance toward a thought not immediately accompanied by instructions for action is founded in fear. Unmanipulated thought and the position that allows nothing to be deduced from this thought must be feared because that which cannot be admitted is perfectly clear: this thought is right"
>
> (Adorno 1991:172).

INTRODUCTION

The argument of this presentation is simple. There can be a *public* sociology only to the extent that it is possible for sociology to appear before audiences that are not exclusively constituted by a professional group that defines itself in terms of the occupation of the institutions and channels of communication of an academic discipline. That would be – and indeed *is* – *private* sociology and invariably of little or no public significance. The indifference that so often greets attempts to publicize the alleged insights of empirical sociological research indicates the telescopic illusion of private sociology. What is important in the journal paper is frequently insignificant outside of the text. A body such as the United Kingdom's Economic and Social Research Council unintentionally shows the prevalence of the telescopic tendency. In a bewildering hall of mirrors it is now funding research into the impact of the research that it funds (Davies, Nutley & Walter 2005). It is worth noting, however, that the non-academic audiences that are assumed by this research on the impact of research are identified as professionals from non-social science backgrounds and policy makers. The over-riding concern is to be 'relevant' to their needs. But if relevance is understood as the ability to give an audience what it wants (that is to say, if relevance means selling knowledge or fetishized methodological competence to a purchaser), there is ultimately the advocacy of nothing more than sociology as 'abstracted empiricism' (Mills 1970). It must be said that the signs are already rife that such sociology is flourishing. It is certainly the case that to be concerned with professional groups and policy makers alone is also to pay little or no attention to the publics of men and women who seek to make sense of their lives because they are human beings in the world with others. This essay takes it as given that these men and women are the only proper publics of sociology, but sociology must be *publicized* if it is to gain quick and immediate access to them, and the problem is that the conditions of publicity are beyond the control of sociology and sociologists.

For the condition of publicity to be achieved in the contemporary social and cultural context it is necessary that sociology be situated within the space of appearances that is provided and constituted by the media. This is a commonplace point, and yet its full implications often fail to be thought through in some of the higher profile discussions of public sociology. For example, Michael Burawoy's (2005) address to the American Sociological Association accepts that public sociology has to appear in the media, but he more or less takes it as given that the news media will report sociological work without distortion and adding their own spins upon it, while publishers will issue books purely because they are of note and quite regardless of sales figures. If the first assumption about news media is naïve and profoundly unsociological, then the second is wishful thinking as everyone will know who has tried to contract a project that is not designed as a student text. Curiously, there seems to be a tendency on the part of some sociologists to pretend that the presentation of their work is immune to the kinds of pressures that sociology has itself shown influences other than knowledge production and dissemination.

The media are considerably more than neutral 'black boxes' that transform into output whatever is put into them, and neither are they a straight conduit through which knowledge flows without obstruction or impediment. They are more appropriately conceived of as an independent *environment* that is oriented around values that are heterogeneous to sociology. As such, if sociology is to appear before publics through the media it will be necessarily shaped by values that are external to it and specific to a heterogeneous environment.

Sociology that is in thrall to the principle of relevance or to the development of data for evidence based policy making – that is to say, abstracted empiricism – is amenable to a situation within the media environment, and indeed desperate for such an acknowledgement of its consequence, because how else might claims to relevance be sustained, and by extension how else might future buyers be found? If the media are the means of publicity then, by definition, any sociology that is not or cannot be situated within the media environment fails any empirical test of relevance and is not put in the market place. This is the nub of the concern of funding bodies such as the Economic and Social Research Council. Bodies such as these are commissioners of research and advertising agencies at one and the same time. This means that sociology desperate to be relevant becomes just one more presence in the already overcrowded media environment and, in the pursuit of a public, has to allow itself to be shaped in its concerns and even determined in its mode of presentation by the heterogeneous values that are the orientations of that environment. Consequently, it can be suggested that public sociology is only possible in as far as sociology is located in a media environment that is not merely alien to it but, more powerfully, actually lethal to the possibilities of sociology, although those with an eye on 'relevance' are unlikely to see the problem in quite this way.

This essay does not seek to overcome that aporia. Rather, it is offered as a contribution to what might be termed a *sociology of paradox*, where the underlying principle is that the promise of sociology consists in an ability to highlight contradictions between social and cultural ideals and practices so that the world might be defamiliarized. In this way a space of possibilities *might* be imaginatively levered open by the clarification of the paradox, thus undermining the common sense that things are as they must be. Here, common sense is understood as the conception of necessity that is promoted by *any* environment. By definition an environment presupposes and promotes the absolute necessity of its own continuation and repudiates as destructive anything that is critical of it. Moreover, and as the word 'environment' implies, any environment is based on a presumption of natural inevitability. It is familiarized as something that life absolutely needs to flourish, and upon that conceit that 'there is no alternative' rests most of its power, and most of the fear of its critique or condemnation.

To occupy the space of the paradox is to avoid giving answers that rationally resolve all disputes. Instead it is deliberately aimed to raise questions by making the world more complex than common sense familiarity permits. This sociology of paradox has its ally not in the provision of 'evidence', policy research or sycophancy but in the literature and cinema that seek to spring the trap of supposed necessity. The spirit and stake of the sociology of paradox is identical with that which Milan Kundera sees in the case of the novel: "Complexity. Every novel says to the reader: 'Things are not as simple as you think'. That is the novel's eternal truth, but it grows steadily harder to hear amid the din of easy, quick answers that come faster than the question and block it off" (Kundera 1988:18).

The media environment is one of the producers of that din and speed, and therefore the possibility of sociology becomes harder to hear precisely as sociology is put before publics in the contemporary social and cultural situation. Let the argument commence.

THE APPEARANCE OF SOCIOLOGY

The question of appearance is taken from Hannah Arendt's discussion of the public realm: "Everything that appears in public can be seen and heard by everybody and has the widest possible publicity", she says. Something 'appears' to the extent that it is capable of "being seen and heard by others as well as ourselves" (Arendt 1958:45). By this definition then, the kind of sociology that remains within the communicative networks of an academic discipline fails the test of being public and of possessing publicity (that is, of being of the public), because it is only seen and heard by the 'ourselves' of professional sociology. This also explains why so much of that private sociology is *incapable* of public appearance even as it becomes more and more intensely pursued by the disciplinary professionals. It becomes a charming and seductive substitute for any encounter with the messiness of human being in the world (hence, therefore, the fondness of private sociology for vast, coherent and ultimately utterly inhuman intellectual systems). Following Arendt it can be argued that in as far as sociology is seen and heard by others who are not within the disciplinary communicative networks (that is, in as far as it appears before others than ourselves), so it is constituted as – and is constitutive of – the worldly reality that is between us and the men and women with whom we enter into relationships. But all the time that sociology remains private it "will always greatly intensify and enrich the whole scale of subjective emotions and private feelings" of its adherents although "this intensification will always come to pass at the expense of the assurance of the reality of the world and men" (Arendt 1958:46). It might therefore be proposed that private sociology is both unreal and reality-denying, all the more keenly it is practised. This observation, of course, compares with C. Wright Mills's essential discovery that there is no necessary connection between prestige as an academic sociologist and possession of a sociological imagination (Mills 1970).

Arendt argues that something can be defined as 'public' to the extent that it is of the world and therefore "common to all of us and distinguished from our privately owned place". Furthermore, "to live together in the world means essentially that a world of things is between those who have it in common" (Arendt 1958:48). If these philosophical underpinnings for a conception of the 'public' are applied to the question of sociology, then they require that at least two conditions must be obtained if there is going to be a public sociology. First of all, sociology that is or wills to be public must make a leap from being a private or personal pursuit and must instead be or be able to become 'common to all of us'. If that condition is to be fulfilled, it requires that sociology is produced with the intention of reaching beyond the academy or specialised publics of professionals and policy makers who are in the market for little more than empirical 'evidence' to justify their own initiatives. It must be a sociology that is open to the world as opposed to a closed system. Second, and following on from that point, any public sociology must be amenable to being something that is between all of us, that belongs to us all and which is therefore a medium through which it is possible for men and women to come together in a world that is constituted in no small degree by the conversations that such sociology stimulates and facilitates. The authorial name indicates merely one author of the texts. By this condition then, public sociology is that which is able to float free of its conditions and intentions of production; public sociology is that which is beyond sociological control. The 'us' is greater than 'ourselves'. A fear of this lack of control is unquestionably one of the most powerful motivating forces of private sociology.

Yet, these conditions also require the achievement of certain *sociological* conditions of existence of public sociology. Quite simply, the conditions of publicity can only be fulfilled if sociology has access to media of communication. There can only be a public sociology if sociology is capable of being made common to all of us, only if it is able to be something between us. Put another way, there can only be a public sociology if publics are able to be or become aware of sociology. There has to be a *space of appearance*.

Hannah Arendt's work points to the identification of that space of appearance with the *polis* where it is through communication that men and women come together on the basis of their plurality, constitute a public through the recognition of a world that is common to them all and express their status as political agents such that the meaning of those things in common and rightful practice in relation to them is agreed. Arendt draws on the ancient Greek tradition that "to live in a *polis*, meant that everything was decided through words and persuasion and not through force and violence" (Arendt 1958:26). But a problem remains. It might well be the case normatively that the things of the world appear in the *polis*, but that still begs the question of *how* that appearance is possible and, indeed, the matter of precisely how the *polis* is constituted in complex societal forms, given that there is not a single geographical or communicative space in which all citizens might gather (the internet does not at all fulfil that condition because access to it is shaped in no small measure by social and cultural capital, and moreover, as a technological form the internet is inherently individualizing). In the contemporary social and cultural context this means that *there can only be a public sociology if sociology appears in the media*.

But what does the term 'the media' mean? The orthodox approaches follow either of two strategies. First, the media are all lumped together into a homogenous ensemble called the 'mass media', with the correlates of mass society or mass culture. The problem here is that the public tends to be taken as constituted rather than constitutive, and this explains why a lot of research in this strategy looks at ideology and so on. The mirror reflection of this approach is to be found in the tendency to celebrate the supposed reflexivity, creativity and polyvocality of media audiences and texts. All that such work achieves is the return of the repressed of the mass media model. Second, the media might be disaggregated into their discrete forms of press, television, radio, cinema and so forth. The problem here is that points of connection between these different forms tend to be identified purely with institutional ownership or specific multi-platform genres and, moreover, any public sense of continuity across the forms tends to get lost or reduced to strategies of 'monetization'. From the point of view of social action, the ownership of media institutions, or their precise technological bases and strategies, are considerably less important than their subjective meaning as constitutive of a more or less seamless series that is embedded in everyday life and which opens up the domestic sphere (where media consumption tends for the most part to take place), to an 'out there' that is likely to be identified as more or less threatening and unintelligible precisely because it undermines the ideational separateness of the domestic. The only alternatives to a sense of threat are seductive entertainment and the embrace of the security blanket of celebrity culture, or, on the other hand, indifference towards an outside world that can never be kept firmly outside. In the modern world of fear and anxiety it is no longer possible to tend only to one's own garden and to stay in a domestic sphere that remains immune to the outside (this is just one of many points that the best film-makers make better than most sociologists; see Ingmar Bergman's *Shame* and Luis Buñuel's *That Obscure Object of Desire* for profound meditations on the impossibility of keeping the outside out).

In view of these kinds of issues, I want to adopt a different approach to the media. Following the work of Roger Silverstone, I contend that in the contemporary social and cultural context, the media is best identified and understood as an *environment*. Silverstone argues that the media 'are becoming environmental' in the sense that they have become inextricably entwined with the practices of everyday life. This has happened to such an extent that contemporary everyday life is unimaginable without the media. They are *environmental* because they are losing any quality that they might once have had of being distinct and are, instead, becoming an intrinsic part of how things are and operate. They are no longer merely *institutions*, any more than are governmental agencies. The media are an environment that is completely part of social and cultural life, even at its most mundane levels. Consequently, they generate and contextualize otherwise impossible practices and transform the same environment that they also constitute (Silverstone 2007:5). It might be said that the media environment is at once structured by and structuring of the world that is presently between us. Building on this foundation, Silverstone contends that the media orient men and women in the world because they facilitate appearance, and (in a remark that is reminiscent of Arendt) he says that "without that appearance the world ... would not exist at all, at least not for us" (Silverstone 2007:6). Indeed, "appearance, mediated appearance ... constitutes our worldliness, our capacity to be in the world" (Silverstone 2007:26). As such the point is that if public sociology is that sociology which is in the world (as opposed to just within the channels of private disciplinary communication), then it must appear, and that appearance has to be within the media environment since that is now the sphere of the constitution of the world and of worldliness.

Yet, Silverstone gets a little carried away with the possibilities of the media environment as a space of appearances. The problems begin when he identifies the media environment with what he calls the *mediapolis*. The word references the media as cultural agents and technologies, as well as Arendt's emphasis upon the *polis* as the space of public appearance, the *polis* as the space of politics that is predicated upon appearance in that space. Silverstone says that "contemporary media enable a face-to-faceness which, both in broadcast and interactive modes (and of course the differences are not insignificant), involves the coming together of speech and action and, albeit in the symbolic realm of mediated representation, they reproduce, though of course in an intensely technologically mediated form, the discursive and judgemental space of the *polis*". In the mediapolis then, the coming together of the plurality of men and women is possible because "the world and its players appear in the media, and for most of us that is the only place they do appear" (Silverstone 2007:30). For 'most of us', it is only in the media environment that sociology appears.

Silverstone acknowledges that some appearances in the mediapolis are vulnerable and tenuous and from that insight he seeks to deduce a recuperative ethics. He embraces *cosmopolitanism* and argues that it is presently viable because globalization "has brought with it an intensification of the condition of the cosmopolitan and an increasing legitimation of the cosmopolitan's status … In the ideal world such a figure is no longer seen as marginal but rather as central to the civic project" (Silverstone 2007:11-12). That civic project

> as an ethic, embodies a commitment, indeed an obligation, to recognize not just the stranger as other, but the other in oneself. Cosmopolitanism implies and requires, therefore, both reflexivity and toleration. In political terms it demands justice and liberty. In social terms, hospitality. And in media terms it requires … an obligation to listen (Silverstone 2007:14).

The ethical role of the media in the context of globalization is then to listen and to make listening possible so that the plurality of men and women might appear in the mediapolis as more or less equal voices, and so that identification with the other (and the other in the self, whatever that means beyond the received wisdom of contemporary theory) might become at once inescapable, desired and desirable. Or at least, that is the perspective from Silverstone's 'ideal world', which is from a sociological point of view little more than wishful thinking.

What does this purported cosmopolitan obligation mean for public sociology? The argument points in one direction that is likely to be followed by many within sociology with considerable enthusiasm. The approach might be used to justify the assertion that sociology is at once the paragon and the harbinger of cosmopolitanism. It is indeed noticeable that cosmopolitanism has been increasingly stressed in the wake of the collapse of socialist hopes and the unthought linkage within so much sociology of politics with platforms. Within contemporary sociology, cosmopolitanism has become a received wisdom because it manages to do a number of things. First, within the context of globalization it enables analysis to be emancipated from an overly common sense identification of societal forms with the nation state. Second, cosmopolitanism enables sociology to speak about ethics without ever having to go to the foundations that sociological dealings with this matter tend to abhor and find so problematic. Ethics becomes about practices of toleration and so on, as opposed to God, nature or some other extra-social or societal (transcendental) category. Cosmopolitanism keeps ethics within the bounds of sociological secular reason (Milbank 1990). These two achievements appear to resolve conceptual, methodological and ethical issues at one and the same time (for an example of this, see Beck 2002). Third, if cosmopolitanism is defined in the way of Silverstone as an 'obligation to listen', then it adds an easy universalism and patina of contemporary relevance to longer standing, and by now hardly controversial, demands to let the silenced speak (although rather often the silenced are only permitted to speak if they can be turned into sociological ventriloquist's dummies). However, it is also very noticeable that the sociological encounters with these issues of cosmopolitanism tend to be taken in a quite technical direction and, thereby, they often become yet one more component of entirely private conversations between 'ourselves'.

But there is another question to ask on the basis of Silverstone's work; a question that is actually a lot more pressing than that of whether or not sociology is cosmopolitan. For the sake of argument, let it be assumed that there is indeed a cosmopolitan quality about sociological work. Let it also be assumed that sociology wishes to be hospitable to a variety of voices in the mediapolis, and that it seeks to encourage and facilitate the discussions of the plurality of men and women. Well, quite simply, all of this can only be achieved if the appearance of sociology in the media environment of the mediapolis is sufficiently powerful to be able to attract those voices and, moreover, secure their allegiance over time. But how can public sociology appear in that way? The answer to that question points to a circularity that is, perhaps, better seen as a spiralling vortex, a trap. Public sociology can only be and promote cosmopolitanism if it is itself an established appearance in the mediapolis, yet it can only be and become such an appearance if it can be accommodated by and within the practices and orientations of the media environment. In short, *the public sociology that is likely to be the most significant from the point of view of cosmopolitanism is likely to be that which is least sociological and most journalistic.*

The Voices of Public Sociology

What needs to be remembered is that fundamentally the media environment is *a sphere of capitalist production and competition*. It is astonishing how easily this simple yet crucial point is forgotten or under-emphasized in so many of the discussions of the ethical possibilities of the media (see, for example, Boltanski 1999). The collapse of socialism is increasingly leading to an analytical blindness to capitalism. Most analysts seem to talk about 'consumerism' nowadays as if it had nothing to do with profit margins, perhaps because what was once just an alternative has now become naturalized (and so, perhaps to this extent at least, Francis Fukuyama's (1993) announcement of the end of history was not as silly as it first seemed, although whether history has ended or simply been abandoned is more than a moot point).

The media environment is one in which different institutions struggle against one another to secure profit by delivering to advertisers or, in the case of state funded bodies such as the BBC, by delivering to regulatory authorities, audience share. This has an impact on the content as well as the institutional forms of the media environment. As Pierre Bourdieu observed: "Through pressure from audience ratings, economic forces weigh on television, and through its effects on journalism, television weighs on newspapers and magazines, even the 'purest' among them .... In this way ... the economy weighs on all fields of cultural production" (Bourdieu 1998:56). From this correct observation it follows that in as far as sociology can only be public if it secures a place in the media, then it can only appear if its presence is economically beneficial – or at least not costly – for the media environment. At worst, sociology must appear in a way that is unthreatening to audiences (as space filler) and, at best, it must be seductive (as reference point). After all, other and competing voices can always be found to fill the spaces that might otherwise be given to sociology, and the space will be readily given if a reallocation is likely to be able to secure a greater audience share. This is the source of the heterogeneous values that shape the appearance of sociology. It also means that the sociology that does so appear is scarcely likely to do what sociology at its most principled can do. Principled sociology seeks to engage us in a conversation that inspires free and autonomous action, and it thereby demonstrates that actually the world could become very different from what is currently is. This presents sociology with a challenge since "questioning and disrupting the routine may not be to everybody's liking" (Bauman 1990:15). It is this challenge that the media environment massages away to the extent that the possibility of the disruption of the routinized and naturalized 'what is' is incompatible with the values that the media environment sustains and makes familiar.

What then are the values of the media environment? This is the point at which Roger Silverstone slips ethical presumptions and assertions into his argument with his talk of an ideal of cosmopolitanism. But following on from Pierre Bourdieu it is possible to develop a different picture of the values that have a performative and presentational impact upon the appearance of public sociology. The concern with audience share that dominates the focus of most media institutions requires that their content must change quickly and easily so that they never become obsolete, boring or unfashionable. The media environment is antithetical to anything that endures over time (anything, that is, except its own profitability). It might be added that this means that the media environment is consequently perfectly oriented towards the structures of consumer capitalism in that both require quick production and quick casting off, with the moment of value being fleeting and in perpetual need of reproduction (compare also with Zygmunt Bauman's discussion of liquid modernity; see Bauman 2000). This has implications for journalistic work and, therefore, for the basis of what appears to audiences. Bourdieu says that journalists are always in a hurry and can never get beneath the surface of a story. They lack sufficient time: "Journalists – the day labourers of everyday life – can show us the world only as a series of unrelated flash photos". Nothing can be allowed to matter too much because within minutes it is likely to be old news, uninteresting, and indeed an impediment to be cast off, since audiences can be best secured through 'scoops' and innovation. Bourdieu continues to say of journalists that "given the lack of time, and especially the lack of interest and information (research and documentation are usually confined to reading articles that have appeared in the press), they cannot do what would be necessary to make events really understandable". Journalists – and by extension this means the media environment in and of itself – cannot take events and make them intelligible by putting them "in a network of relevant relationships". Consequently, the world becomes absurd, dehistoricized and dehistoricizing (Bourdieu 1998:7).

Yet, in as far as the world becomes absurd and unintelligible, it also becomes existentially threatening to and for men and women, and so they retreat further and further into the "haven in a heartless world" (Lasch 1995) of the domestic sphere, only for that escape route to be undermined every time there is engagement with the media environment, as there necessarily will be in the quest for entertainment. The result is that if audiences are going to continue to engage with the media environment (and thus enable the capitalist institutions of that environment to secure the audience share that is sold to advertisers or regulators), that environment must be able to negate the threats that it otherwise creates. First of all, there will be a subordination of news to the entertainment genre and, second, the absurdity of the world will be turned into a mere surface confusion through the construction of narratives that resolve conflict and make everything orderly (or at least intelligible) once again. The world, in other words, will be re-naturalized.

These are the circumstances in which sociology appears in the media environment, and in which it is allowed to appear because it is an easy way in which journalistic production can intimate depth beneath surfaces and networks of connection between what are otherwise presented as like flash photos. In other words, sociology appears in the media environment in as far as it promises to make the connections between events that journalistic production itself – with its perpetual concern with the reproduction of the new – has neither time nor inclination to pursue. *Sociology appears in the media environment because it is a convenient way of making the world safe and sensible.* From this it follows that there are three dominant voices with which sociology speaks in the media environment: as *information*, as *expert knowledge* and as *opinion*. In order to speak with one of these voices, sociology allows itself to be subordinated to values and orientations that are profitable for the media environment and yet destructive for the quality of sociological analysis.

Information is the product of research that is concerned with 'relevance' and with the production of evidence for policy makers. Information is *disseminated*, and external writers put it into a narrative (that is, others transform it into something that is available and meaningful to 'us'). In the media environment this specifically means that journalists use sociology in order to add an evidently evidential base or air of empirical validity to their own positions. Madeleine Bunting of *The Guardian* is an exemplar of this strategy, whereby the sociological producer of information becomes significantly less important in constructing meaning than the journalist who provides and even imposes the narrative upon the data (for one instance of her style, see Bunting 2007. However, it ought to be noted that without Bunting sociological literacy in the United Kingdom would be much lower than it is).

Expert knowledge consists in the sociology that is used in the media environment in order to provide an ostensive explanation for the social event or phenomenon in question. The implication is that sociology in the guise of social science can provide an objective explanation for why something happens and in the way that it does. The conceit of expert knowledge is far more dangerous to sociology than the voice of information. This is because it leads enquiry down each of the three blind alleys that John Carroll identified as the causes of the paucity of so much sociology. Carroll puts the case in his characteristically elegant prose, and he says of the sociologist (as an ideal typical figure) that "the three investments that have carried him astray are science, idealism, and social relevance. They have made him uninteresting, except in the eyes of other parvenus, who, when true to type, are blind to all but the glitter of their own tinsel" (Carroll 1980:2). These 'other parvenus' would include the journalists and the various producers of the media environment. Expert knowledge rests its credibility on claims to scientificity that themselves tend to be reducible to methodological fetishism. Idealism is bolstered because the expertise is invariably presented in reports that end with grandly confident statements of the order of "what is needed is....". Social relevance meanwhile is frequently taken to be either self-evident because the issue under consideration must be relevant or else the experts would not be interested in it, or because the matter at hand is validated by absorption within the media environment. It is noticeable that both of these justifications for social relevance are halls of mirrors, just like the concern to fund research into the impact of funded research (and of course the research on the research will also be the concern of funded research in due course).

Opinion has a certain allure because it flatters the ideal of cosmopolitanism. To the extent that sociologists are given the opportunity to write opinion pieces in broadsheet newspapers or feature on 'serious' current affairs programmes, they are appearing within the media environment before an audience that is considerably greater than that of 'ourselves' and moreover, they are being put into debate with other, competing, positions. In this way, there can be, and ostensibly is, practical communication in terms of plurality and the constitution of an 'us'. However, sociology only appears as opinion on account of the qualities of the sociologist, and not on account of what it is that they are seeking to communicate to and with audiences. Here, the point to remember is that opinion pieces are *commissioned* by the institutions of the media environment and only exceptionally rarely *volunteered*. This raises the question of the criteria that an individual must meet if they are going to receive an invitation. First, they must possess a certain cultural capital. This capital can be derived from identification with a body of expert knowledge or, more likely, academic position, communicative and performative competence and, certainly in the case of the British media environment, often a measure of exoticism. This explains why in the United Kingdom it is considerably easier to be given a place in the media environment if one's academic affiliation is, say, the London School of Economics than, say, Wolverhampton. Second, the sociologist must be identified as having something to say. In the media environment this invariably means that sociology becomes a participant in *controversy* or, to recall Carroll, the statement of a platforming idealism. In its worse guise it appears as contrarianism. Although she is not a sociologist, Germaine Greer is the best illustration of this criterion in the British media environment. Third, the sociologist must be able to communicate in the style that the relevant media institution requires and has made familiar to its target audience. Given the speed and perpetual out-of-dateness of the content of the media environment, this means that the sociological (perhaps it is better called the sociologist's) opinion must be amenable to a prose style of short sentences and brief paragraphs, and nuance has to be subordinated to assertion. The structuring of voice within the media environment thus requires that complex points cannot be made, or at least can only be made if they are severely banalized. Here I will not give illustrative examples of sociologists who are evidently able to communicate in this way. If these different aspects that can be considered under the heading of *opinion* are pulled together, they suggest that if sociology appears as an opinion piece beneath the name of a sociologist, then that sociologist has been chosen to give an opinion because he or she possesses qualities that are deemed valued by the media environment. Put another way, they play the game.

These are the three *dominant* voices with which sociology speaks in the media environment. Yet, despite their failings they are also the three best voices with which sociology can reach and speak in that environment. After all, there is a fourth voice, and it is very disturbing. *Sociology can also appear as entertainment*. The entertainment factor is based on a distortion of the ability of sociology to reveal otherwise hidden worlds. In principled sociology the intention of that revelation is to connect personal troubles with public issues (so that it becomes clear that 'this is not just happening to me' but is constitutive of 'us'), and politically it reflects a concern to render visible what common sense and naturalizing institutions seek to hide away. But as soon as revelation is made within the media environment, it is transformed. The media environment operates according to a cultural logic that assumes that everything is susceptible to being made visible to audiences. That logic takes the human world away from human relationships. Its forms and relationships are reified so that they become 'things' to be found; they are naturalized and turned into an 'is' that is more or less exotic. It is thanks to their inability to withstand exoticization that these otherwise hidden human worlds are attractive to the institutions of the media environment. Yet, if they are left to remain as exotic, these worlds might also be threatening to individualized media audiences, and this is the point at which sociology comes to speak with the voice of entertainment. First, the exoticism can be made safe through the adoption of a sociological voice that slips between the inquisitive and the sardonic; between the 'why are these people doing that?' to the 'what peculiar things are done by these people who are so different to ourselves – what is being done by *them*?'. Second, the exoticism can become a playground for sociological adventures. For example, a BBC programme has featured a relatively esteemed sociologist driving with friends through a British city and commenting with good humour on the different 'urban tribes' that are to be seen. When others are exoticized and turned to objects of entertainment, they are also made completely safe: "They are no longer images of another way of life but rather freaks or types of the same life, serving as an affirmation rather than negation of the established order" (Marcuse 1968:60). The irony is that the entertaining sociologists become freaks in exactly this way too; they affirm what they purport to expose. The question is why are some sociologists keen to become entertainers? The answer is depressingly obvious. They are seduced by the glitter of their own tinsel (and the fees that are paid by the media institutions) and yet explain it all away as proof of their 'relevance'.

The implication is clear; sociology can appear before publics if it accepts domination and distortion by the heterogeneous values of the media environment; yet in that acceptance sociology is also required to become a performer in the capitalistic search for audiences. This sociology reduces human freedom. As Herbert Marcuse once said in a different yet entirely consonant context: "Proclaiming the existing social reality as its own norm, this sociology fortifies in the individuals the 'faithless faith' in the reality whose victims they are" (Marcuse 1968:102).

Conclusion

Sociology is trapped in a paradox that cannot be willed away all the time that attempts are made to appear before publics. The nub of the paradox is this: public sociology is a pawn in the capitalistic struggles of the media environment and therefore subject to heterogeneous values that it cannot withstand. Meanwhile, private sociology can go its own way, but only at the expense of never appearing before publics. But perhaps even there the effects of the media environment are not too far away. As Pierre Bourdieu observes: "Given the tendency of the media today to celebrate market products designed for the best-seller lists ... young poets, novelists, sociologists, and historians, who sell three hundred copies of their books are going to have a harder and harder time getting published" (Bourdieu 1998:58). The result of this is the emergence of what amounts to an academic celebrity culture and the stunting of the new generations. New voices can only appear if they write for a ready made audience within the community of 'ourselves' and thus fall into the traps of abstracted empiricism, grand theory or platforming, or if they seek a fast-track to celebrity by talking about the fashionable (but in the end that is merely the fast-track to obsolescence).

Undoubtedly, one answer that will be given to this paradox is that public sociology nevertheless can still appear and be worthwhile thanks to the strategic expedient of the avoidance of the media environment and, instead, willing insinuation in a micro-politics of civil society. Yet, that is no answer at all since the existence of civil society is something that can be no longer presumed. Indeed, the inability to take civil society for granted is one of the deeper worries of the discussion about social capital. The concern about the evident decline of social capital can be read as an elegy to civil society, even though it tends to take all three of the blind alleys signposted by John Carroll (Putnam 2001). More importantly, however, the logic of the media environment is that it has colonized or replaced what could be previously identified as civil society. The kinds of campaigning groups with which any sociology in and of civil society would presumably be keen to be working are engaged in the struggle to do nothing less than secure appearance in the media. The argument for public sociology through civil society merely removes to one degree the problem of the media environment and does not at all constitute any kind of resolution.

Is this a counsel of despair? Not at all, but we need to think within the paradoxes of public sociology and be brave enough with our careers to avoid the tinsel of private sociology. Despair can be avoided if the focus of attention is always resolutely on the reasons why sociology is important and, to put the matter more subjectively, why the sociology bug bit us in the first place. Speaking for myself, I can recall my first encounters with sociology. There was a profound feeling that all of a sudden I was reading my biography. But it was not *my* biography at all; it was *our* biography, it belonged to *us*. Admittedly, not all sociology had this impact, but the work that did had been written in terms of a commitment on the part of the sociologist to certain principles that they never allowed to be compromised. These works levered possibility out of entrapment because they were concerned with human freedom and autonomy, not personal prestige. I saw 'us' thanks to these works of *principle*. I saw 'us' emerge from the ruins of the familiar. In the end, it is a question of *vocation*.

I propose that sociology is most likely to play a part in the constitution of 'us' if the struggle to appear in the media is given up, and if there is a refusal to collaborate ('collaboration' is Bourdieu's word; see Bourdieu 1998:59) with the media environment. Indeed, it is not at all unreasonable to suggest that the best way of achieving a public sociology might well be to give up on the task of trying to achieve a public sociology. If we sociologists work according to the guiding principles of human freedom and autonomy, at least we will have made a distinctively free and human contribution to the world. Will publics come to us or is our autonomous activity fated to be met with indifference and ignorance? Those are precisely *not* the questions with which we ought to be concerned. Publics will coalesce around sociology or they will not. After all, to promote human freedom is also to promote the freedom to ignore sociology (and to expect or demand an audience is a denial of freedom and therefore precisely unprincipled). What we need to do is produce principled work that is hard to ignore once it is discovered. This would be work that is hard to ignore not because of appearance in the media environment, but because of its unflinching commitment to human values and to the social and societal forms that are necessary if men and women are going to be secure enough to accept their freedom and autonomy. Publics will make public sociology or they will not, and it is the role of the sociologist to leave to those potential publics something of principle around which they *might* form, something in which they *might* find value.

The only right route to the achievement of a *public* sociology is commitment to the vocation of a *principled* sociology.

REFERENCES

Adorno, Theodor W. (1991): *The Culture Industry: Selected Essays on Mass Culture*. London: Routledge.

Arendt, Hannah (1958): *The Human Condition: A Study of the Central Dilemmas Facing Modern Man*. New York: Doubleday.

Bauman, Zygmunt (1990): *Thinking Sociologically*. Oxford: Blackwell.

Bauman, Zygmunt (2000): *Liquid Modernity*. Cambridge: Polity Press.

Beck, Ulrich (2002): "The Cosmopolitan Society and its Enemies". *Theory, Culture & Society*, 19 (1-2):17-44.

Benjamin, Walter (1973): *Illuminations*. London: Fontana.

Boltanski, Luc (1999): *Distant Suffering: Morality, Media and Politics*. Cambridge: Cambridge University Press.

Bourdieu, Pierre (1998): *On Television and Journalism*. London: Pluto Press.

Bunting, Madeleine (2007): "Capital Ideas". *The Guardian*, 18 July.

Burawoy, Michael (2005): "For Public Sociology". *American Sociological Review*, 76 (1):4-28.

Carroll, John (1980): *Sceptical Sociology*. London: Routledge & Kegan Paul.

Davies, Huw, Sandra Nutley & Isabel Walter (2005): *Approaches to Assessing the Non-Academic Impact of Social Science Research*. http://www.esrc.ac.uk/ESRCInfoCentre/Images/non-academic_impact_symposium_report_tcm6-16593.pdf.

Fukuyama, Francis (1993): *The End of History and the Last Man*. Harmondsworth: Penguin Books.

Kundera, Milan (1988): *The Art of the Novel*. London: Faber & Faber.

Lasch, Christopher (1995): *Haven in a Heartless World: The Family Besieged*. New York: W.W. Norton.

Marcuse, Herbert (1968): *One Dimensional Man: The Ideology of Industrial Society*. London: Sphere.

Milbank, John (1990): *Theology and Social Theory: Beyond Secular Reason*. Oxford: Blackwell.

Mills, Charles Wright (1970): *The Sociological Imagination*. Harmondsworth: Penguin Books.

Putnam, Robert (2001): *Bowling Alone: The Collapse and Revival of American Community*. New York: Simon & Schuster.

Silverstone, Roger (2007): *Media and Morality: On the Rise of the Mediapolis*. Cambridge: Polity Press.

PUBLIC SOCIOLOGY AS SUBJECT MATTER OF SOCIOLOGY

~

Michael Hviid Jacobsen

THE PROLIFERATION OF PUBLIC SOCIOLOGY

In recent years, many pieces of academic or scholarly work have been devoted to and published dealing with sociology and its relationship to the public. The reason for this torrential publishing frenzy on public sociology may be many. One could, for example, point to a 'crisis' in sociology's relationship with the public as one possible explanation – that the gradual withdrawal and alienation of sociology from the public now culminates in a counter-movement materialising in writings about how to escape such a crisis situation. An alternative explanation could be that sociology, together with most other academic disciplines, increasingly has to legitimate its funding and its raison d'être by proving its usefulness and relevancy to the public, broadly understood. From a Danish perspective, most of these pieces, however, have been published abroad and the discussion of 'public sociology' – sometimes referred more specifically to as 'critical sociology' or 'applied sociology' – has so far predominantly been an Anglo-American phenomenon instigated particularly by Michael Burawoy's presidential address to the American Sociological Association in 2004 which, however, intensified the debate in the subsequent years culminating with at least five international book titles published since then explicitly devoted to the topic and several in journal symposia mentioned in the introduction to this book – and this is more likely than not only the top of the iceberg.

However, there has been some sort of time-lag throughout the rest of the world regarding adopting the agenda of discussing public sociology, but we are – perhaps – gradually witnessing a proliferation of the discussion of public sociology also elsewhere – in Denmark most recently in debates in the media as well as in academic journals over normative, critical and public sociologies by representatives of the discipline. No doubt the years to come will prove that debates on the public relevancy of sociology are far from a geographically limited matter. It is, I believe, a universal feature – an inherent aspect – of thinking about and practicing sociology.

Due to the blurred boundaries between scholarly work dealing explicitly with public sociology on the one hand and pieces published touching upon it only more implicitly on the other, the lists compiled of recommended reading provided below are not intended to be all-inclusive or exhaustive; they are merely indicative and suggestive of where the interested reader may find further inspiration and insight when writing on or debating the issue of public sociology. They are, as it were, the beginning not the end for thinking about and carrying out public sociology. Moreover, the heaps of work published on public sociology, especially in recent years, are constantly growing. Most books on or within sociology in fact deal either explicitly or implicitly with sociology's role and its repercussions or functions in connection to the wider society. One might even say suggest that the 'suffering' of sociology perhaps consists in its constant preoccupation with its own scientific status and social usability. The lists below therefore merely aspire to point readers to some classic as well as more recent pieces of work that sprung to my mind when conceiving this book. Thus, it represents a selective reading and sometimes even a random scanning of the field of public sociology – and naturally mirrors my own training and my own preoccupations.

It is my hope that the idea and notion of public sociology will not continue to be an almost purely unpublic (that is sociologically and academically introvert) preoccupation and pastime but that it – in the future – may prove to be something not merely preached but also practiced. Public sociology is not only something to be discussed, not merely something to be theorised or thought about – it is, perhaps first and foremost, something to be done, something to be carried out. Thus, I end this book on public sociology by passing on the baton to the readers.

RECOMMENDED BOOKS AND REPORTS

Agger, Ben (2000): *Public Sociology: From Social Facts to Literary Acts*. Lanham, MD: MA: Rowman & Littlefield.

ASA Task Force on Institutionalizing Public Sociologies (2005): *Public Sociology and the Roots of American Sociology: Re-Establishing Our Connections to the Public*. Available at http://pubsoc.wisc.edu/e107_files/public/tfreport090105.pdf.

Blau, Judith & Keri E. Iyall Smith (eds.)(2006): *Public Sociologies Reader*. Lanham, MD: Rowman & Littlefield.

Clawson, Dan et al. (eds.)(2007): *Public Sociology: Fifteen Eminent Sociologists Debate Politics and the Profession in the Twenty-First Century*. Berkeley, CA: University of California Press.

Fairchild, Henry Pratt (1920): *Outline of Applied Sociology*. New York: Macmillan.

Flyvbjerg, Bent (2001): *Making Social Science Matter: Why Social Inquiry Fails and How It Can Succeed Again*. Cambridge: Cambridge University Press.

Gibbons, Michael et al. (1994): *The New Production of Knowledge*. London: Sage Publications.

Gouldner, Alvin W. (1973): *For Sociology*. New York: Basic Books.

Gouldner, Alvin W. & Seymour M. Miller (eds.)(1965): *Applied Sociology: Opportunities and Problems*. New York: Free Press.

Habermas, Jürgen (1971): *Knowledge and Human Interests*. Boston: Beacon Press.

Halliday, Terence C. & Morris Janowitz (eds.)(1992): *Sociology and Its Publics: The Forms and Fates of Disciplinary Organization*. Chicago: University of Chicago Press.

Horowitz, Irving L. (1994): *The Decomposition of Sociology*. New York: Oxford University Press.

Lee, Alfred McClung (1986): *Sociology for Whom?* Syracuse: Syracuse University Press.

Lynd, Robert S. (1939/1970): *Knowledge for What? – The Place of Social Science in American Culture*. Princeton: Princeton University Press.

MacRae, Donald G. (1976): *The Social Function of Social Science*. New Haven: Yale University Press.

Mills, Charles Wright (1959): *The Sociological Imagination*. New York: Oxford University Press.

Nichols, Lawrence C. (ed.)(2007): *Public Sociology: The Contemporary Debate*. New York: Transaction Publishers.

Phillips, Derek L. (1971): *Knowledge From What?* Chicago: Rand McNally & Company.

Reda, Mario R. (2005): *Public Sociologies: A Looking Glass for What Could Be*. Boston: Allyn & Bacon.

Scott, Robert A. & Arnold R. Shore (1979): *Why Sociology Does Not Apply? – A Study of the Use of Sociology in Public Policy*. New York: Elsevier.

Simey, T. S. (1968): *Social Science and Social Purpose*. London: Constable.

Steele Stephen F. & Jammie Price (2003): *Applied Sociology: Topics, Terms, Tools, and Tasks*. London: Wadsworth Publishing.

Turner, Stephen P. & Jonathan H. Turner (1990): *The Impossible Science: An Institutional Analysis of American Sociology*. Newbury Park, CA: Sage Publications.

Wallerstein, Immanuel et al. (1996): *Open Up the Social Sciences: Report of the Gulbenkian Commission of the Restructuring of the Social Sciences*. Stanford, CA: Stanford University Press.

Wilson, William J. (ed.)(1993): *Sociology and the Public Agenda*. Thousand Oaks, CA: Sage Publications.

Znaniecki, Florian (1940): *The Social Role of the Man of Knowledge*. New York: Harper.

Recommended Articles

Acker, Joan (2005): "Comments on Burawoy on Public Sociology". *Critical Sociology*, 31 (3):327-331.

Bauman, Zygmunt (1998): "Sociological Enlightenment – For Whom, About What?". *Dansk Sociologi*, 9 (special issue):43-54.

Beck, Ulrich (2005): "How Not To Become a Museum Piece". *British Journal of Sociology*, 56 (3):335-343.

Brady, Advid (2004): "Why Public Sociology May Fail". *Social Forces*, 82 (4):1629-1638.

Braithwaite, John (2005): "For Public Social Science". *British Journal of Sociology*, 56 (3):345-353.

Burawoy, Michael (2004): "Public Sociology: Contradictions, Dilemmas and Possibilities". *Social Forces*, 82 (4):1603-1618.

Burawoy, Michael (2005): "2004 ASA Presidential Address – For Public Sociology". *American Sociological Review*, 70 (1):4-28.

Burawoy, Michael (2005): "For Public Sociology". *British Journal of Sociology*, 56 (2):259-294.

Burawoy, Michael (2005): "The Return of the Repressed: Recovering the Public Face of U.S. Sociology, One Hundred Years On". *Annals of the American Academy of Political and Social Science*, 600 (1):68-85.

Burawoy, Michael (2005): "Response: Public Sociology: Populist Fad or Path to Renewal?". *British Journal of Sociology*, 56 (3):417-432.

Burawoy, Michael, William Gamson, Charlotte Ryan, Stephen Pfohl, Diane Vaughan, Charles Derber & Juliet Schor (2004): "Public Sociologies: A Symposium from Boston College". *Social Problems*, 51 (1):103-130.

Calhoun, Craig (2005): "The Promise of Public Sociology". *British Journal of Sociology*, 56 (3):355-363.

Ericson, Richard (2005): "Publicizing Sociology". *British Journal of Sociology*, 56 (3):365-372.

Etzioni, Amitai (2005): "Bookmarks for Public Sociologists". *British Journal of Sociology*, 56 (3):373-378.

Gans, Herbert (2002): "More of Us Should Become Public Sociologists". *ASA Footnotes* at http://www.asanet.org/footnotes/julyaugust02/fn10.html.

Ghamara-Tabrizi, Behrooz (2005): "Can Burawoy Make Everybody Happy? Comments on Public Sociology". *Critical Sociology*, 31 (3):361-369.

Hadas, Miklós (2007): "Much Ado About Nothing? Remarks on Michael Burawoy's Presidential Address". *American Sociologist*, 38 (3):309-322.

Hall, John A. (2005): "A Guarded Welcome". *British Journal of Sociology*, 56 (3):379-381.

Holmwood, John (2007): "Sociology as Public Discourse and Professional Practice: A Critique of Michael Burawoy". *Sociological Theory*, 25 (1):46-66.

Hu, Linda (2007): "Doing Public Sociology in the Field – A Strong Sociology Intervention Project in China". *American Sociologist*, 38 (3):262-287.

Johnson, Paul (2004): "Making Social Science Useful". *British Journal of Sociology*, 55 (1):23-30.

Kalleberg, Ragnvald (2000): "The Most Important Task of Sociology is to Strengthen and Defend Rationality in Public Discourse". *Acta Sociologica*, 43 (4):399-411.

Kalleberg, Ragnvald (2005): "What Is 'Public Sociology'? Why and How Should It be Made Stronger?". *British Journal of Sociology*, 56 (3):387-393.

Light, Donald W. (2005): "Contributing to Scholarship and Theory through Public Sociology". *Social Forces*, 83 (4):1647-1654.

Nielsen, Francois (2005): "The Vacant 'We': Remarks on Public Sociology". *Social Forces*, 82 (4):1619-1627.

Ortiz, Steven M. (2007): "Breaking Out of Academic Isolation: The Media Odyssey of a Sociologist". *American Sociologist*, 38 (3):223-249.

Piven, Francis Fox (2004): "Sociology Needs a Public", in *An Invitation to Public Sociology* (edited by the American Sociological Association). Washington D.C.: American Sociological Association.

Quah, Stella R. (2005): "Four Sociologies, Multiple Roles". *British Journal of Sociology*, 56 (3):395-400.

Ritzer, George (2006): "Who's a Public Intellectual?". *British Journal of Sociology*, 57 (2):209-213.

Rule, James B. (1978): "Models of Relevance: The Social Effects of Sociology". *American Journal of Sociology*, 84 (1):78-98.

Scott, John (2005): "Who Will Speak, and Who Will Listen? Comments on Burawoy and Public Sociology". *British Journal of Sociology*, 56 (3):405-409.

Sheiring, Gábor (2007): "Barbarians at the Open Gates: Public Sociology and the Late Modern Turn". *American Sociologist*, 38 (3):294-308.

Strydom, Piet (1999): "Triple Contingency: The Theoretical Problem of the Public in Communication Societies". *Philosophy & Social Criticism*, 25 (2):1-25.

Tittle, Charles R. (2004): "The Arrogance of Public Sociology". *Social Forces*, 82 (4):1639-1643.

Turner, Bryan S. (2006): "Public Intellectuals, Globalization and the Sociological Calling: A Reply to Critics". *British Journal of Sociology*, 57 (3):345-351.

Wimberley, Ronald C. & Libby V. Morris (2007): "Communicating Research to Policymakers". *American Sociologist*, 38 (3):288-293.

Wolfe, Alan (1992): "Weak Sociology/Strong Sociologists: Consequences and Contradictions of a Field in Turmoil". *Social Research*, 59 (4):759-779.

Recommended Websites

Public sociology: http://en.wikipedia.org/wiki/Public_sociology

PublicSociology.com

Save Sociology: www.cas.sc.edu/socy/faculty/deflem/Savesociology/02publicsociology.html

List of Contributors

Ottar Brox (b. 1932), received his PhD in Rural Sociology at the Norwegian College of Agriculture in 1970, Assistant Professor of Social Anthropology, University of Bergen, 1969-1971, Professor of Sociology, University of Tromsø 1972-1984 and Senior Researcher at the Norwegian Institute of Urban and Regional Research in Oslo, 1984-2001. On leave as Member of the Norwegian Parliament 1973-1977 for Sosialistisk Venstreparti. Brox conducted fieldwork in northern Norway, Newfoundland and Chile and has published approximately twenty books. Among these are: *Hva skjer i Nord-Norge? En studie i norsk utkantpolitikk* [*What Happens in North Norway? A Study of Norwegian Periphery Policies*] (1966), *Newfoundland Fishermen in the Age of Industry: A Sociology of Economic Dualism* (1972), *Arbeidskraftimport: Velferdsstatens redning eller undergang?* [*Import of Labour: The Salvation or Destruction of the Welfare State?*] (2005) and *The Political Economy of Rural Development* (2006).

Henrik Dahl (b. 1960), writer and chief analyst at Explora A/S (a research company specializing in applied social science). Dahl has written numerous books on historical, political and social matters. His most well-known book is *Hvis din nabo var en bil* [*If Your Neighbour Were A Car*] (1997), a study seeking to validate Mary

Douglas's group/grid theory with hard data. Moreover, he has written other titles such as *Den kronologiske uskyld* [*The Chronological Innocence*] (1998) and *Krigeren, borgeren og taberen* [*The Warrior, the Citizen and the Loser*] (with Ole Thyssen, 2006). His most recent book is *Den usynlige verden* [*The Invisible World*] (2008) on the neglected and despised spaces such as gas stations, train stations, freeways and suburbs.

Bent Flyvbjerg (b. 1952), Professor of Planning at Aalborg University, Denmark, and Chair of Infrastructure Policy and Planning at Delft University of Technology, the Netherlands. He was twice a Visiting Fulbright Scholar to the US, where he did research at UCLA, UC Berkeley and Harvard University. His books include: *Rationality and Power: Democracy in Practice* (1998), Making Social Science Matter (2001), *Megaprojects and Risk: An Anatomy of Ambition* (with Nils Bruzelius & Werner Rothengatter, 2003) and *Decision-Making on Megaprojects* (with Hugo Priemus & Bert van Wee, 2008). His books and articles have been translated into 18 languages.

Michael Hviid Jacobsen (b. 1971), Associate Professor, PhD and Director of Studies of Sociology, Aalborg University, Denmark. For several years he has written on everyday life sociology and conducted studies especially of death and dying with an everyday life perspective. Publications include: *The Transformation of Modernity* (edited with Mikael Carleheden, 2001), *Erving Goffman* (with Søren Kristiansen, 2002), *Bauman Before Postmodernity* (with Keith Tester, 2005), *Bauman Beyond Postmodernity* (with Sophia Marshman & Keith Tester, 2007), *The Sociology of Zygmunt Bauman* (edited with Poul Poder, 2008), *The Sociologies of the Unnoticed* (edited, 2008) and *The Contemporary Goffman* (edited, forthcoming).

James B. Rule (b. 1943) was educated at the University of California, Brandeis University and Harvard University, where he received his PhD in Sociology in 1969. He has had teaching and research appointments at MIT, Nuffield College (Oxford), the Universite de Bordeaux, Clare Hall (Cambridge) and at the State University of New York. He is currently Distinguished Affiliated Scholar at the Center for Law and Society, University of California, Berkeley. He has held fellowships from the Guggenheim Foundation, the Center for Advanced Study in the Behavioral Sciences at Stanford, the Institute for Advanced Study at Princeton, the Russell Sage Foundation and other institutions. He is author of seven books, including studies of privacy, civil violence, progress in social science and the role of social inquiry in social betterment as well as numerous articles in international journals. His books include the following titles: *Measuring Political Upheaval* (with Charles Tilly, 1964), *Private Lives and Public Surveillance* (1973), *Insight and Social Betterment* (1978), *The Politics of Privacy* (with Doug McAdam, Linda Stearns & David Uglow, 1988) and *Theory and Progress in Social Science* (1997). His latest book is *Privacy in Peril* (2007).

Keith Tester (b. 1960), Professor of Cultural Sociology at the University of Portsmouth, United Kingdom, and Distinguished Visiting Fellow at the Thesis Eleven Centre for Critical Theory, LaTrobe University, Australia. His books include: *Civil Society* (1992), *The Inhuman Condition* (1995), *Moral Culture* (1997), *Compassion, Morality and the Media* (2001), *Conversations with Zygmunt Bauman* (2001), *The Social Thought of Zygmunt Bauman* (2004), *Bauman Before Postmodernity* (with Michael Hviid Jacobsen, 2005), *Bauman Beyond Postmodernity* (with Michael Hviid Jacobsen & Sophia Marshman, 2007) and the latest *Eric Rohmer: Film as Theology* (2008).